# 777 GREAT CLEAN JOKES

## A Sparkling Collection of Unsullied Humor

JENNIFER HAHN

BARBOUR
PUBLISHING

© 2006 by Barbour Publishing, Inc.

ISBN 1-59789-126-6

All rights reserved. No part of this publication may be repro-
duced or transmitted for commercial purposes, except for brief
quotations in printed reviews, without written permission of
the publisher.

Churches and other noncommercial interests may reproduce
portions of this book without the express written permission
of Barbour Publishing, provided that the text does not exceed
500 words or 5 percent of the entire book, whichever is less,
and that the text is not material quoted from another publisher.
When reproducing text from this book, include the following
credit line: "From *777 Great Clean Jokes*, published by Barbour
Publishing, Inc. Used by permission."

Cover image © iStockphoto

Published by Barbour Publishing, Inc., P.O. Box 719,
Uhrichsville, Ohio 44683 www.barbourbooks.com

*Our mission is to publish and distribute inspirational products
offering exceptional value and biblical encouragement to the masses.*

Printed in the United States of America.
5 4 3 2 1

# CONTENTS

ANIMALS . . . . . . . . . . . . . . . . . . . . . 5

BUSINESS AND JOBS . . . . . . . . . . . . . . 46

CHURCH AND FAITH . . . . . . . . . . . . 71

EDUCATION . . . . . . . . . . . . . . . . . . . . . 93

ELECTRONICS AND MECHANISMS . . . . 114

FAMILY MATTERS . . . . . . . . . . . . . . . . 122

FINANCES . . . . . . . . . . . . . . . . . . . . . . 132

FOOD . . . . . . . . . . . . . . . . . . . . . . . . . 138

HISTORY . . . . . . . . . . . . . . . . . . . . . . . 145

LAW AND ORDER . . . . . . . . . . . . . . . 151

LOVE AND MARRIAGE . . . . . . . . . . . . 168

MEDICINE . . . . . . . . . . . . . . . . . . . . . . 174

MUSICAL NOTES . . . . . . . . . . . . . . . . 188

POTPOURRI . . . . . . . . . . . . . . . . . . . . . 191

SENIOR MOMENTS . . . . . . . . . . . . . . . 200

SPACE AND NATURE . . . . . . . . . . . . . . 206

SPORTS AND LEISURE . . . . . . . . . . . . . 214

TRAVEL AND TRANSPORTATION . . . . 236

# ANiMALS

## 1

Hickory dickory dock,
The mice ran up the clock,
The clock struck one,
And the others escaped with minor injuries.

## 2

What keys can't open locks?
*Monkeys, donkeys, and turkeys.*

## 3

Why did Mozart sell his chickens?
*They kept saying, "Bach, Bach, Bach."*

## 4

Some Boy Scouts from the city were on a camping trip. The mosquitoes were so fierce, the boys had to hide under their blankets to avoid being bitten. Then one of the scouts saw some lightning bugs and said to his friend, "We might as well give up. They're coming after us with flashlights."

## 5

My cat is so smart. He eats cheese, then waits at the mouse hole with baited breath.

## 6

Boy: Could you sell me a shark?
Pet-shop owner: Why do you want a shark?
Boy: My cat keeps trying to eat my goldfish, and I want to teach him a lesson.

## 7

Frank: Did you hear about the guy who was arrested at the zoo for feeding the pigeons?
Harry: No. What's wrong with feeding the pigeons?
Frank: He fed them to the lions.

## 8

If baby pigs are called piglets, why aren't baby bulls called bullets and baby chickens chicklets?

## 9

What is the difference between a cat and a match?
*A cat lights on its feet, and a match lights on its head.*

## 10

What grows up while it grows down?
*A baby duckling.*

## 11

What's gray on the inside and clear on the outside?
*An elephant in a sandwich bag.*

## 12

Why do dragons sleep during the day?
*So they can hunt knights.*

## 13

Why is a snake so smart?
*Because you can't pull its leg.*

## 14

Why do giraffes have such small appetites?
*Because with them, a little goes a long way.*

## 15

What is as big as an elephant but doesn't weigh an ounce?
*An elephant's shadow.*

## 16

What did the boy octopus say to the girl octopus?
*"Can I hold your hand, hand, hand, hand, hand, hand, hand, hand?"*

## 17

A cowboy had two horses, but he couldn't tell them apart. He cut off one horse's mane, but it grew back; he cut off the tail, but that grew back, too. A friend suggested that he measure the horses. The cowboy measured them and went to his friend and said, "That was a great idea—the black one was two inches taller than the white one."

## 18

Heading into the jungle on his first safari, the American visitor was confident he could handle any emergency. He sidled up to the experienced native guide and said smugly, "I know that carrying a torch will keep lions away."

"That's true," the guide replied. "But it depends on how fast you carry the torch."

## 19

A mother's bachelor son invited her over for a meal. He had just gotten two new dogs and wanted his mom to see them.

When she sat down at the table, she noticed that the dishes were the dirtiest that she had ever seen in her life. "Have these dishes ever been washed?" she asked, running her fingers over the grit and grime.

"They're as clean as soap and water could get them," he answered. She felt a bit apprehensive but started eating anyway.

The food was really delicious, and she said so, despite the dirty dishes.

When dinner was over, her son took the dishes, put them on the floor, whistled, and yelled, "Here, Soap! Here, Water!"

## 20

First octopus: What do *you* like least about being an octopus?
Second octopus: Washing my hands before dinner.

## 21

Two hens were pecking in the yard when suddenly a softball came sailing over the fence, landing a few feet away from them. One hen said to the other, "Will you just look at the ones they're turning out next door!"

## 22

Several buffalo were grazing on the prairie when a cowboy rode up. Looking at the animals, he said disgustedly, "You are the ugliest buffaloes I've ever seen. Your fur is matted, you have humps on your backs, and you're slobbering all over the place."

The cowboy turned and rode off, and one buffalo said to another, "I think I just heard a discouraging word."

## 23

Steve: How did your parakeet die?
Fred: Flu.
Steve: Don't be silly. Parakeets don't die from the flu.
Fred: Mine did. He flew under a bus.

## 24

Which is richer, a bull or a cow?
*A bull. The cow gives you milk; the bull charges you.*

## 25

How many skunks does it take to smell up a neighborhood?
*Just a phew.*

## 26

City slicker: I finally went for a ride this morning.
Ranch hand: Horseback?
City slicker: Yep, he got back about an hour before I did.

## 27

What is a polar bear's favorite place to vacation?
*Brrr-muda.*

## 28

What is a woodpecker's favorite kind of joke?
*A knock-knock.*

## 29

What is an eel's favorite card game?
*Glow Fish.*

## 30

Why did the turtle go to the therapist?
*He wanted to come out of his shell.*

## 31

How does a beaver know which tree to cut down?
*Whichever one he chews.*

## 32

What would you call a snake that drinks too much coffee?
*A hyper viper.*

## 33

What would you get if you crossed a baseball player with a frog?
*An outfielder who catches flies and then eats them.*

## 34

What kind of flowers would you give an absent-minded squirrel?
*Forget-me-nuts.*

## 35

What do you get if Bach falls off a horse, but has the courage to get on again and continue riding?
*Bach in the saddle again.*

## 36

How do pigs say good-bye?
*With hogs and kisses.*

## 37

What is an owl's favorite mystery?
*A whooo-dunit.*

## 38

A man was driving past a farm and saw a three-legged chicken running alongside his car. Suddenly, the chicken picked up speed and disappeared around the bend. The driver pulled to the side of the road and called to the farmer, "I just saw a three-legged chicken!"

"Oh, yes," said the farmer. "We have a bunch of 'em. We have three people in our family, and we all like drumsticks."

"Well, how do they taste?" asked the motorist.

"Dunno," said the farmer. "We can't catch any."

## 39

Three mice are sitting around boasting about their strengths. The first mouse says, "Mouse traps are nothing! I do push-ups with the bar."

The second mouse pulls a pill from his pocket, swallows it, and says with a grin, "That was rat poison."

The third mouse got up to leave. The first mouse says, "Where do you think you're going?"

"It's time to go home and chase the cat."

## 40

"Have you got any kittens going cheap?" asked a customer in a pet shop.

"No, sir," replied the owner. "All our kittens go, 'Meow.'"

## 41

"Look over there!" said the frightened skunk to his pal. "There's a human with a gun, and he's getting closer and closer! What are we going to do?"

The second skunk bowed his head and calmly replied, "Let us spray."

## 42

Two goats wandered into the junkyard and had a field day. One of them spent a particularly long time bent over a reel of film. When he was finished, the other goat came over. "So, did you enjoy the film?"

The goat replied, "To tell you the truth, I liked the book better."

## 43

One day a chicken went to a library and said, "Book, book, book." The librarian gave the chicken three books, and the chicken went on its way.

The next day the same chicken came into the library and said, "Book, book, book." So the librarian gave the chicken three books again, but this time she became suspicious of where the chicken was taking the books, so she decided to follow the chicken.

After awhile, the chicken came to a swamp and stopped beside a frog. The chicken gave the three books to the frog, and the frog said, "Read it! Read it! Read it!"

## 44

What did the snail say when he hitched a ride on the turtle?

*"Wheeeee!"*

## 45

"Look at that speed!" said one hawk to another as a jet-fighter plane zoomed over their heads.

"Hmph!" snorted the other. "You would fly fast, too, if your tail was on fire!"

## 46

A hound dog and a dalmatian were sitting in an Internet café. The dalmatian said to the hound, "Hey, check out my Web site!"

The hound asked for the address, and the dalmatian responded, "www.dalmatian.dot-dot-dot-dot-dot-dot-dot-dot."

## 47

What do you call a story told by a giraffe?
*A tall tale.*

## 48

One ant was running across an unopened box of crackers and urging another to speed up.

"But why do we have to hurry?" asked the other.

"Can't you read? It says, 'Tear along the dotted line.'"

## 49

Two fleas were walking out of a theater when they discovered it was raining hard.

"Shall we walk?" said one flea.

"No," said the other. "Let's take a dog."

## 50

Why are frogs so happy?
*They eat whatever bugs them.*

## 51

What does a bankrupt frog say?
*"Baroke, baroke, baroke."*

## 52

Did you hear about the skunk that went to church?
*He had his own pew.*

## 53

What animal has more lives than a cat?
*A frog, because he croaks every night.*

## 54

A chicken walks into a restaurant.

The hostess says, "We don't serve poultry!"

The chicken says, "That's okay; I just want a soda."

## 55

A hungry lion was roaming through the jungle, looking for something to eat. He came across two men. One was sitting under a tree reading a book; the other was typing away on his laptop. The lion quickly pounced on the man reading the book and devoured him.

Even the king of the jungle knows that readers digest, and writers cramp.

## 56

When you call a dog, he usually comes to you.
When you call a cat, he takes a message.

## 57

Chicken to turkey: Only Thanksgiving and Christmas? You're lucky; with us, it's any Sunday.

## 58

Two guys were hiking in the forest when they suddenly came across a big grizzly bear. The one guy took off his hiking boots and put on some running shoes. His friend said to him, "You're crazy! Don't you know how fast grizzlies are? You'll never be able to outrun it!"

"Outrun it?" said his friend. "I only have to outrun you!"

## 59

Why are anteaters so healthy?
*Because they are high on ant-i-bodies!*

## 60

Why did the chicken cross the road?
*To show the opossum it could be done.*

## 61

One caterpillar to another, as they watch a butterfly:
You'll never get me up in one of those things.

## 62

Exasperated dragon on the field of battle:
Mother said there would be knights like this.

## 63

Where does a cat go when he loses his tail?
*A retail store.*

## 64

Did you hear the Energizer Bunny was arrested?
*He was charged with battery.*

## 65

Where are dogs scared to go?
*The flea market.*

## 66

Why did the parrot wear a raincoat?
*She wanted to be polyunsaturated.*

## 67

Why was the cat afraid of the tree?
*Because of its bark.*

## 68

Turtle to turtle: Don't you just love the sound of
rain on your roof?

## 69

Why do lobsters have a hard time sharing?
*Because they're shellfish.*

## 70

What's the difference between a cat and a comma?
*A cat has its claws at the end of its paws; a comma is a
pause at the end of a clause.*

## 71

"Jenny!" called her mother, "Why are you feeding
birdseed to the cat?"

"I have to," Jenny replied. "That's where my
canary is."

# 72

A mother mouse and a baby mouse were walking along, when all of a sudden, a cat attacked them. The mother mouse yelled, "Bark!" and the cat ran away.

"See?" said the mother mouse to her baby. "Now do you see why it's important to learn a foreign language?"

# 73

Have you heard about the dog that ate an onion?
*Its bark was much worse than its bite.*

# 74

A cowboy rides into town on Friday, stays three days, and leaves on Friday. How does he do it?
*His horse's name is Friday.*

# 75

Two cows are standing in a wide-open field. One cow says to the other cow, "Hey, are you worried about that mad cow disease?"

The second cow says, "Why would I be worried about mad cow disease? I'm an airplane!"

## 76

Did you hear the one about the lion who ate clowns?
*You'll roar.*

## 77

What do you call an overweight cat?
*A flabby tabby.*

## 78

What is worse than a giraffe with a sore neck?
*A centipede with athlete's foot.*

## 79

What did the five-hundred-pound canary say as he
walked down the street?
*"Here, kitty, kitty, kitty."*

## 80

What do you call a cat that's been thrown in the dryer?
*Fluffy.*

## 81

What do you call a cat that gets thrown in the dryer and is never found again?
*Socks.*

## 82

What do you call a grizzly bear with no teeth?
*A gummy bear.*

## 83

What do you get when you put a bird in the freezer?
*A brrrd.*

## 84

When is fishing not a good way to relax?
*When you're the worm.*

## 85

Why can't you play hide-and-seek with poultry in a Chinese restaurant?
*Because of the Peking duck.*

## 86

A turtle was mugged by three snails, but when a police officer asked the turtle to give a description of what happened, all he could say was, "I don't know, Officer. It all happened so fast!"

## 87

What do you call a fish with no eye?
*A fsh.*

## 88

Who's a better boxer, a bean or a chicken?
*The bean—he's no chicken.*

## 89

What is a shark's favorite game?
*Swallow the Leader.*

## 90

What do pigs put in their hard drives?
*Sloppy disks.*

## 91

Baby snake: Mom, are we poisonous?
Mom snake: We most certainly are! Why?
Baby snake: I just bit my tongue.

## 92

Why did the kangaroo lose the basketball game?
*He ran out of bounds.*

## 93

What birds spend time on their knees?
*Birds of prey.*

## 94

What do you get when you cross an elephant with a kangaroo?
*Big holes all over Australia.*

## 95

What's the difference between a soccer player and a dog?
*The soccer player wears a team uniform, the dog just pants.*

## 96

What do you get when you cross a bunny rabbit with the World Wide Web?
*A hare Net.*

## 97

At the end of his shift, the police officer parked his police van in front of the station. His K-9 partner, Bo, was in the back.

As the officer was exiting his car, a little boy walked by and looked in the back window of the van.

"Is that a dog you got back there?" the boy asked.

"It sure is," the officer replied.

Puzzled, the boy looked at the officer, then back at the van. Finally he said, "What did he do?"

## 98

Why are elephants known to hold grudges?
*They can forgive, but they can't forget.*

## 99

Did you hear about the duck that was flying upside down?
*It quacked up.*

# 100

Where do fish like to go on vacation?
*Finland.*

# 101

How do you find a spider on the Internet?
*Check out his Web site.*

# 102

What do you call a penguin in the desert?
*Lost.*

# 103

The farmer's son was returning from the market with a crate of chickens his father had entrusted to him, when all of a sudden the box fell and broke open.

Chickens scurried off in different directions, but the boy walked all over the neighborhood, retrieving the birds and returning them to the repaired crate. Hoping he had found them all, the boy returned home.

"Pa, the chickens got loose," the boy told his father reluctantly, "but I managed to find all nine of them."

"You did well, son," the farmer said, "because you left with only six."

# 104

Tony was having trouble getting his neighbor to keep his chickens fenced in. The neighbor kept talking about chickens being great creatures, and as such, they had the right to go wherever they wanted.

On his next trip to the grocery store, Tony bought a dozen eggs. That night, he snuck out and placed the eggs throughout his yard.

The next morning, when he was sure the neighbor was watching, Tony went out and gathered the eggs.

After that, he never had problems again with finding his neighbor's chickens in his yard.

# 105

Why did the giraffe graduate early?
*He was head and shoulders above the rest.*

# 106

Where do polar bears vote?
*The North Poll.*

# 107

What did Winnie the Pooh pack for his vacation?
*The bear essentials.*

## 108

How did the owl with laryngitis feel?
*He didn't give a hoot.*

## 109

What does an educated owl say?
*"Whom."*

## 110

What should you do when someone throws a goose at you?
*Duck.*

## 111

What do you say when someone throws a duck at another duck?
*"Duck, duck!"*

## 112

What do you say when someone throws a goose at a duck?
*"Duck, duck! Goose!"*

## 113

What bird is always out of breath?
*A puffin.*

## 114

A young bird fell out of its nest and hurtled through the branches of the tree, heading for the ground.

"Are you all right?" called out a robin as the chick zoomed by.

"So far!" said the little bird.

## 115

Teacher: Where are elephants found?
Student: They're so big, I didn't think they could get lost!

## 116

Have you heard the story about the peacock that crossed the road?
*It really is a colorful tail. . . .*

## 117

A husband and wife were on a safari in Africa. A huge lion suddenly leaped out in front of them and seized the wife in its jaws.

"Shoot!" she screamed to her husband. "Shoot!"

"I can't, dear!" he hollered back. "I'm all out of film!"

## 118

What's the difference between a tiger and a lion?
*The tiger has the mane part missing.*

## 119

How does a leopard change its spots?
*When it's tired of one spot, it just moves to another.*

## 120

What goes "peck, bang, peck, bang, peck, bang"?
*A bunch of chickens in a yard full of balloons.*

## 121

Where do little dogs sleep when they go camping?
*In pup tents.*

## 122

What bone will a dog never eat?
*A trombone.*

## 123

A German shepherd went to the telegraph office to send a telegram. "Woof," he wrote. "Woof. Woof. Woof. Woof. Woof. Woof. Woof. Woof."

The clerk looked at the message and said, "There are only nine words here. You could add one more 'Woof' for the same price."

"But," said the dog, "then it wouldn't make any sense at all."

## 124

What wears a coat in the winter and pants all summer?
*A dog.*

## 125

What did the dalmatian say after he finished eating?
*"That hit the spots."*

## 126

How do you find your dog if he's lost in the woods?
*Put your ear up to a tree and listen for the bark.*

## 127

Where do fish take a bath?
*In a river basin.*

## 128

What animal makes it hard to carry on a conversation?
*A goat, because he always wants to butt in.*

## 129

What did one horse say to the other horse?
*"Your pace is familiar, but I don't remember your mane."*

## 130

What happens if pigs fly?
*Bacon goes up.*

# 131

The door to the Pony Express office swung open. A cowboy sprinted out, took a running leap, and landed in the middle of the road.

"What's the matter with you, pardner?" asked a bystander. "Did they throw you out, or are you just crazy?"

"Neither," replied the cowboy. "But just wait until I find out who moved my horse!"

# 132

How do you catch a unique rabbit?
*Unique up on it.*

# 133

How do you catch a tame rabbit?
*Tame way. Unique up on it.*

# 134

What was the snail doing on the highway?
*About a mile a day.*

## 135

What is the best advice you can give to a worm?
*"Sleep late!"*

## 136

What do you get when you cross a hen with a hyena?
*An animal that laughs at every yolk.*

## 137

What do you get when you cross a pig and a centipede?
*Bacon and legs.*

## 138

What do you call a dog with a receding hairline?
*Bald Spot!*

## 139

A man dressed in camouflage entered a butcher shop. "I'd like a couple of ducks," he said.

"We're out of ducks. I have a couple of nice chickens, though."

"Chickens!" the man exclaimed. "I can't tell my wife I bagged a couple of chickens!"

# 140

A man ran up to a farmhouse and pounded on the door. When the farmer came to the door, the man demanded, "Where's the nearest train station, and what time is the next train to the city?"

The farmer replied, "You may cut through my field, and you should reach the station in time for the 5:20. But if my bull sees you, you'll probably make it by 5:00."

# 141

Swimmer: Are you sure there aren't any sharks along this beach?

Lifeguard: Oh, yes, I'm sure. They don't get along well with the alligators.

# 142

"My dog has no tail," said one man to another out walking his dog.

"Oh, that's too bad," the other replied. "How do you know when he is happy then?"

"He stops biting me!"

# 143

"Your horse is very well behaved," the lady noted to the resting rider.

"Oh, that's true," he replied. "When we come to a fence, he always stops quickly and lets me go over first!"

# 144

What happens when a frog's car breaks down?
*He gets toad away.*

# 145

What do you call two spiders who just married?
*Newlywebs.*

# 146

What do you call the best butter on the farm?
*A goat.*

# 147

What do you call a cow that has just given birth?
*De-calfinated.*

# 148

Two elephants were discussing life in general on Earth.

"You know," said one, "humans say that we possess the best memories of any animals on the globe."

"Well," said the other, "why can't I remember where I left my bag of peanuts?"

# 149

What kind of can never needs a can opener?
*A pelican.*

# 150

What did the pink rabbit say to the blue rabbit?
*"Cheer up!"*

# 151

What do you get when you cross a pig and a tree?
*A porky pine.*

# 152

Why do white sheep eat more grass than black sheep?
*Because there are more of them.*

## 153

Why shouldn't you tell a pig a secret?
*Because he's a squealer.*

## 154

What do frogs want to listen to at bedtime?
*Croak-and-dagger stories.*

## 155

What is cowhide most used for?
*Holding cows together.*

## 156

What kind of snake is good at math?
*An adder.*

## 157

What do you give a deer with an upset stomach?
*Elk-a-seltzer.*

## 158

Eggs and ham: A day's work for a chicken, a lifetime commitment for a pig.

## 159

Why does a mother kangaroo hope it doesn't rain?
*She doesn't like it when the kids have to play inside.*

## 160

How do you fix a broken chimp?
*With a monkey wrench.*

## 161

What do llamas like to eat?
*Llama beans.*

## 162

What do you call a time-out in the Lions' football game?
*A paws.*

## 163

What did the mother buffalo say to her boy as he was leaving?

*"Bison."*

## 164

What kind of snack do little monkeys have with their milk?

*Chocolate chimp cookies.*

## 165

What did the teddy bear say when he was offered dessert?

*"No thanks. I'm stuffed."*

## 166

How does an octopus go into battle?

*Fully armed.*

## 167

What kind of money do marsupials use?

*Pocket change.*

# 168

One evening as a mother was preparing dinner, her seven-year-old son came down to the kitchen, crying hysterically. The loving mother bent down and said, "Honey, what's wrong?"

"Mom," he said, "I just cleaned my room."

"Well, I'm very proud of you," she replied. "But why on earth would that make you cry?"

Her son looked up through his tears and said, "Because I still can't find my snake!"

# Business
## and Jobs

## 169

Ed: I have a job in a watch factory.
Mike: Oh really? What do you do?
Ed: I just stand around and make faces.

## 170

Farmer: Quite a storm we had last night.
Neighbor: Yep, it sure was.
Farmer: Did it damage your barn any?
Neighbor: I dunno. I haven't found it yet.

## 171

Employee: I've worked here for over twenty years
and have never asked for a raise.
Employer: That's why you've worked here for twenty
years.

## 172

Salesman: You make a small down payment, but then
you don't make any payments for six months.
Customer: Who told you about me?

# 173

How is business?
    Tailor: Oh, it's so-so.
    Electrician: It's fairly light.
    Author: All right.
    Farmer: It's growing.
    Astronomer: Looking up!
    Elevator operator: Well, it has its ups and
        downs.
    Trash collector: It's picking up.

# 174

Employee: My wife says I should ask you for a raise.
Employer: I'll ask my wife if I can give you one.

# 175

Wife: You don't look well. What's the matter?
Husband: You know those aptitude tests we give our
    employees?
Wife: Yes.
Husband: Well, I took one today, and it's a good
    thing I own the company.

## 176

Barber: Your hair is getting thin.
Client: Who wants fat hair?

## 177

Employer: I thought you requested yesterday afternoon off to go see your dentist.
Employee: Yes, sir.
Employer: Then why did I see you coming out of the stadium with a friend?
Employee: That was my dentist.

## 178

Rancher: What kind of saddle do you want? One with or without a horn?
Cowboy: Without is fine. There doesn't seem to be much traffic around here.

## 179

Dan: I just finished a long run on Broadway.
Zach: What play were you in?
Dan: Oh, I wasn't in any play. A mugger chased me for ten blocks.

## 180

Television repairman: So, what seems to be the problem with your television?

Woman: It has double images. I hope you men can fix it.

## 181

A husband raced into his house. "I've found a great job!" he exclaimed to his wife. "The pay is incredible, they offer free medical insurance, and give three weeks' vacation!"

"That does sound wonderful," said the wife.

"I'm glad you think so," replied her husband. "You start tomorrow."

## 182

A Texan was on a flight and began bragging about the property that he owned.

"How much property do you own?" asked the man sitting next to him.

"Forty acres," answered the Texan.

"That doesn't sound like all that much," replied the man. "Where is this property located?"

"Oh," said the Texan, "downtown Dallas."

# 183

Why was the employee fired from the orange juice factory?
*He couldn't concentrate.*

# 184

Barber: Sir, could you please turn the other side of your face toward me?
Client: Oh, you're finished shaving this side already?
Barber: Oh, no. I just don't like the sight of blood.

# 185

The CEO of a large corporation was in a meeting with the board of directors. He presented his plan, although he knew that several of the board would disagree.

"All in favor, say, 'Aye,'" said the CEO. "All opposed, say, 'I resign.'"

# 186

Why do bakers work so hard?
*Because they need the dough.*

# 187

First cowboy: Why did you carry only one log for the campfire when the other hands carry two?
Second cowboy: I guess the others are too lazy to make two trips.

# 188

The captain of a cavalry fort was having breakfast when his lieutenant ran in the door.

"Captain," he said with a salute, "we've just received an urgent letter from our desert outpost. It states their dire need of water."

"The water supply should arrive there in a few days. They can wait," said the captain.

"Sir, I don't believe so," the lieutenant replied. "The stamp was attached to the envelope with a paper clip."

# 189

Why did the archaeologist go bankrupt?
*Because his career was in ruins.*

## 190

A man was interviewing for a job. "And remember," said the interviewer, "we are very keen about cleanliness. Did you wipe your shoes on the mat before entering?"

"Oh, yes, sir," replied the man.

The interviewer narrowed his eyes and said, "We are also very keen about honesty. There is no mat."

## 191

Why did the doughnut maker retire?
*He was fed up with the hole business.*

## 192

The shopkeeper was discouraged when a new business much like his own opened up next door and erected a huge sign that read, BEST DEALS.

He was depressed when another competitor opened up on the block and announced its arrival with an even larger sign reading, LOWEST PRICES.

The shopkeeper was panicked until he got an idea. He put the biggest sign of all over his own shop—it read, MAIN ENTRANCE.

## 193

A store manager overheard one of his salesmen talking to a customer. "No, sir," said the salesman. "We haven't had any for a while, and it doesn't look like we'll be getting any soon."

The manager was horrified and immediately called the salesman over to him. "Don't you ever tell a customer we're out of anything! Now, what did he want?"

"Rain," answered the salesman.

## 194

Two barbershops were in red-hot competition. One put up a sign advertising haircuts for seven dollars. His competitor put up one that read, WE REPAIR SEVEN-DOLLAR HAIRCUTS.

## 195

During a training exercise, an army unit was late for afternoon inspection.

"Where are those camouflage trucks?" the irate colonel barked.

"They're here somewhere," replied the sergeant, "but we can't find 'em."

## 196

Why did the farmer receive an award?
*Because he was outstanding in his field.*

## 197

On the way to preschool, the doctor let his daughter look at his stethoscope. His little daughter picked it up and began playing with it. This thrilled the father as he thought, *Perhaps one day she will follow in my footsteps and become a doctor.*

But then he heard her as she spoke into the instrument, "Welcome to McDonald's. May I take your order?"

## 198

A little girl asked her mother for fifty cents to give to an old lady in the park. Her mother was touched by the child's kindness and gave her the required sum.

"There you are," said the mother. "But tell me, isn't the lady able to work anymore?"

"Oh yes," came the reply. "She sells candy."

# 199

A salesman telephoned a household, and a four-year-old answered.

Salesman: May I speak to your mother?

Child: She's not here.

Salesman: Well, is anyone else there?

Child: My sister.

Salesman: Okay, fine. May I speak to her?

Child: I guess so.

There was a long silence on the other phone. Then. . .

Child: Hello?

Salesman: It's you. I thought you were going to get your sister.

Child: I did. The trouble is, I can't lift her out of the playpen.

# 200

A man asked the barber, "How much for a haircut?"

"Eight dollars," said the barber.

"And how much for a shave?"

"Six dollars."

"Okay, then, shave my head."

# 201

Who is the best-paid employee at Microsoft?
*The Windows washer.*

## 202

Do you know why electricians are some of the smartest people?
*They always keep up with current events.*

## 203

How did the scientist invent bug spray?
*She started from scratch.*

## 204

What did the astronaut think of the takeoff?
*She thought it was a blast.*

## 205

What do you need to know to be an auctioneer?
*Lots.*

## 206

Boss: You should have been here at 9:30 a.m.
Employee: Why, what happened?

## 207

A young executive was preparing to leave the office late one evening, when he found the CEO standing in front of a shredder with a piece of paper in his hand.

"This is a very sensitive and important document," said the CEO, "and my secretary has gone for the night. Can you get this thing to work for me?"

"Certainly," said the young executive eagerly. He turned the machine on, inserted the paper, and pressed the START button.

"Excellent! Thank you!" said the CEO, as his paper disappeared inside the machine. "I just need one copy. . . ."

## 208

A blacksmith finished hammering a white-hot horseshoe and threw it down on the ground to cool.

Just then a man walked in, spotted the horseshoe, and picked it up. He quickly dropped it, biting his tongue to keep from screaming.

"Pretty hot, huh?" asked the blacksmith.

"Nah," answered the man. "It just doesn't take me long to look over a horseshoe."

## 209

The factory foreman inspected the shipment of crystal vases ready to leave the plant and approached his new packer. "I see you did what I asked: stamped the top of each box, THIS SIDE UP, HANDLE WITH CARE."

"Yes, sir," the worker replied. "And just to make sure it arrives safely, I stamped it on the bottom, too."

## 210

A manager got stuck in the elevator, between floors. After some banging, he finally attracted attention. His name was taken and rescue promised.

It took two hours for the elevator mechanic to arrive and get the manager out. When he returned to his desk, he found this note from his efficient secretary: "The elevator people called and will be here in two hours."

## 211

"I have just developed the most powerful acid compound known to mankind," a scientist told her colleagues. "There is only one problem."

"What is that?" asked one.

"I can't find a container for it," she replied.

## 212

The manager of a glass and window company advertised in the paper for experienced glaziers. Since a good glass man is hard to find, he was pleased when a man who called about the job said he had twelve years of experience.

"Where have you worked as a glazier?" the manager asked.

The man replied, "Krispy Kreme."

## 213

The interviewer examined the job application, then turned to the prospective employee.

"I see you have put ASAP down for the date you are available to start. However, I see you've written down AMAP for required salary. I don't believe I'm aware of what that means."

The applicant replied, "As Much As Possible!"

## 214

A politician asked a minister, "What is something the government can do to help the church?"

"Well," the minister replied, "quit making one-dollar bills."

## 215

There was a captain of a ship who carried around a mysterious black box. Despite repeated questions from his crew, he refused to tell anyone what was inside the box. Years went by, and the mystery of the box grew and grew. It was all the crew could talk about. What was in that mysterious black box?

One day a big storm quickly approached. The wind howled, and the ship was tossed on huge waves. Suddenly, a wave washed across the deck and swept the captain overboard. He disappeared from view and was never seen again.

As soon as the storm passed, a sailor went to the captain's cabin and retrieved the box. The entire crew circled around as he opened it and removed the only contents, a small piece of paper.

On the paper was written, "Starboard is right, port is left."

## 216

"I think I deserve a raise," the man said to his boss. "You know there are three other companies after me."

"Is that right?" asked the manager. "What other companies are after you?"

"The electric company, the phone company, and the gas company."

## 217

Two gas company servicemen were out checking meters in a suburban neighborhood. They parked their truck at the end of the alley and worked their way to the other end. At the last house, a woman watched out her kitchen window as they checked her gas meter.

When they were finished checking the meter, the older of the two challenged his younger coworker to a race back to the truck.

As they came running up to the truck, they realized a woman was huffing and puffing right behind them. They stopped and asked her what was wrong.

In between breaths, she explained, "When I saw the two of you check my meter, then take off running, I figured I'd better run, too!"

## 218

An employee went to see his supervisor. "Boss," he said, "we're doing some heavy housecleaning at home tomorrow, and my wife asked me to help with the attic and the garage, moving and hauling stuff."

"We're shorthanded," the boss replied. "I can't give you the day off."

"Thank you," said the employee. "I knew I could count on you!"

## 219

The owner of a large factory decided to make a surprise visit and check up on his staff. As he walked through the plant, he noticed a young man doing nothing but leaning against the wall. He walked up to the young man and said angrily, "How much do you make a week?"

"Three hundred bucks," replied the young man.

Taking out his wallet, the owner counted out three hundred dollars, shoved it into the young man's hands, and said, "Here is a week's pay—now get out and don't come back!"

Turning to one of the supervisors, the owner asked, "Just how long had that lazy kid been working here?"

"He doesn't work here," said the supervisor. "He was just here delivering our pizzas."

## 220

The manager is reviewing a potential employee's application and notes that the fellow has never worked in retail before.

"For a man with no experience," he says, "you are certainly asking a high wage."

"Well, sir," the applicant replies, "the work is much more difficult when you don't know what you're doing."

## 221

A veteran of World War II applied for a job at a bank. The impersonal interviewer continued to ask question after question, scribbling notes and never looking at the veteran.

"Most recent position?" asked the official.

"Supply officer," replied the applicant.

"Duration of employment?"

"Three and a half years."

"Reason for termination?"

The applicant stopped and thought for a moment, then answered, "We won."

## 222

A young man was a slow worker and found it difficult to hold down a job. After a visit to the employment office, he was offered work at the local zoo.

When he arrived for his first day, the keeper, aware of his reputation, told him to take care of the tortoises.

Later, the zookeeper dropped by to see how the young man was doing and found him standing by an empty enclosure with the gate open. "Where are all the tortoises?" he demanded.

"I can't believe it," said the new employee. "I just opened the door and *whooosh*, they were gone!"

## 223

When his printing ink began to grow faint, a man called a local repair shop. The friendly salesperson who answered the phone said the printer would probably only need to be cleaned. Because the store charged fifty dollars for the cleaning, he advised the caller that he might be better off reading the printer's manual and trying to clean the machine himself.

Pleasantly surprised by his candor, the caller asked, "I don't think your boss would like that you're discouraging business, would he?"

"It's actually my boss's idea," the employee admitted. "He says we usually make more money on repairs if we let people try to fix their equipment first."

## 224

Burt had a problem with oversleeping and was always late for work. His boss threatened to fire him if he didn't do something about it. So Burt went to his doctor, who gave him a pill and told him to take it before he went to bed.

Burt slept incredibly well; in fact, he woke up before the alarm went off. He had a leisurely breakfast and a pleasant ride to work.

"Boss," he said, "that pill my doctor prescribed actually worked!"

"That's great," said the boss, "but where were you yesterday?"

## 225

A guy walks into the human-resources department of a large company and hands the executive his application. The executive begins to scan the sheet and sees that the applicant has been fired from every job he has ever held.

"I have to say," says the executive, "your work history is awful. You've been terminated from every job."

"Yes," says the man.

"Well," continues the executive, "there isn't much positive about that!"

"Sure there is," says the applicant. "I'm not a quitter!"

## 226

Betty was looking for a new RN position, as she was unhappy with her current job. She was certain she'd have no trouble finding a new position, due to the extent of the nursing shortage in her area.

She e-mailed cover letters to dozens of potential employers and attached her resume to each one. Three weeks later, Betty was wondering why she had not received even one request for an interview.

Finally she received a message from a prospective employer that gave an answer to the dilemma. It read: "Your resume was not attached as stated. I do, however, want to thank you for the wonderful fettuccine alfredo recipe."

## 227

A site foreman had ten very lazy men working for him, so one day he decided to trick them into doing some work for a change.

"I have a really easy job today for the laziest one among you," he announced. "Will the laziest man please raise his hand."

Nine hands shot up.

"Why didn't you put your hand up?" he asked the tenth man.

"It was too much trouble."

## 228

A young businessman had just started his own firm. He had leased a beautiful office and had it furnished with antiques. Sitting behind his desk, he saw a man come into the outer office. Wishing to appear busy, the businessman picked up the phone and started to pretend he had a big deal working.

Finally, he hung up and asked the visitor, "May I help you?"

"Sure," the man said. "I've come to hook up your phone!"

## 229

The boss called one of his employees into the office. "Rob," he said, "you've been with the company for six months. You started off in the mailroom. Just one week later, you were promoted to a sales position, and one month after that you were promoted to district sales manager. Just four months later, you were promoted to vice president. Now it's time for me to retire, and I want you to take over the company. What do you say to that?"

"Thanks," said the employee.

"Thanks?" the boss replied. "That's all you can say?"

"Oh, sorry," the employee said. "Thanks, Dad."

## 230

How did the carpenter break his teeth?
*He chewed on his nails.*

## 231

A man applied for a job at a construction firm.

"We take turns making the coffee," said the foreman. "Do you know how to make coffee?"

"I sure do," said the applicant.

"And can you drive a forklift?"

"Why? Just how big is the coffee maker?"

## 232

Job seeker: I'm here in reply to your ad for a handyman.
Potential employer: And you are handy?
Job seeker: Couldn't be handier. I live right next door.

## 233

Herb had spent all afternoon interviewing for a new job. He began by filling out all the papers. The human-resources manager then questioned him at length about his training and past work experience. Herb then was given a tour of the plant and was introduced to the people he would be working with.

Finally, he was taken to the general manager's office. The manager rose from his chair, shook his hand, and asked him to sit down.

"You seem to be very qualified," he said, "and we would like you to come work for us. We offer a good insurance plan and other benefits. We will pay you six hundred dollars a week starting today and in three months, we'll raise it to seven hundred dollars a week. When would you like to start?"

"In three months," Herb replied.

## 234

What training do you need to be a garbage collector?
*None; you just pick it up as you go along.*

## 235

The new ensign was assigned to submarines, his dream since he was a young boy.

He was trying to impress the master chief with his expertise learned in sub school.

The master chief cut him off quickly and said, "Listen, it's really simple. Add the number of times we dive to the number of times we surface. Divide that number by two. If the result isn't an even number, don't open the hatch."

## 236

A man at the construction site was bragging that he was stronger than anyone else. He began making fun of one of the older workmen. After several minutes, the older worker had had enough.

"I'll bet that I can haul something in a wheelbarrow over to the other building that you won't be able to wheel back."

"Okay," the young man replied. "Let's see what you've got."

The older man reached out and grabbed the wheelbarrow by the handles. Then he looked at the young man and said with a smile, "All right. Get in."

# Church and Faith

## 237

Sunday school teacher: Who lived in the Garden of
　　Eden?
Danny: The Adams.

## 238

Grandma: Were you a good girl at church today,
　　Missy?
Missy: Yes, I was. When the nice man offered me a
　　whole plate of money, I said, "No, thank you."

## 239

Why didn't they play cards on Noah's ark?
*Because Noah sat on the deck.*

## 240

Sunday school teacher: Why did Moses wander in
　　the desert for forty years?
Ginny: Because he was too stubborn to stop and ask
　　for directions?

## 241

Sunday school teacher: Phil, who was the first woman?
Phil: I don't know.
Sunday school teacher: I'll give you a hint. It had something to do with an apple.
Phil: Oh, I know. Granny Smith!

## 242

The preacher stopped in the middle of his powerful sermon to ask, "Who is God, anyway?"

From the back of the church, a little boy said, "God is a chauffeur."

"Why do you say that?" asked the preacher.

"Because," said the boy, "he drove Adam and Eve out of the Garden of Eden."

## 243

A teacher asked the kindergartners, "Can a bear take off his warm overcoat?"

"No," they answered.

"Why not?"

Finally, after a long silence, a little fellow spoke up. "Because only God knows where the buttons are."

## 244

A Sunday school class was ready for its question-and-answer session.

"What is it that we learn from Jonah and the whale?" asked the teacher.

A bright kid spoke up and said, "What we learned is that people make whales sick."

## 245

A Sunday school teacher asked her class, "What did Jesus say about people getting married?"

Little Johnny quickly answered, "Jesus said, 'Father, forgive them, for they know not what they do.'"

## 246

The young couples' Sunday school class was studying the story of Abraham and Sarah, who in their nineties were blessed with a child. Among other things, the teacher asked, "What lesson do we learn from this story?"

A young mother of three who was having financial difficulties blurted out, "They waited until they could afford it!"

# 247

A father was teaching his son to admire the beauties of nature.

"Look, son," he exclaimed, "isn't that sunset a beautiful picture God has painted?"

"It sure is, Dad," responded the youngster enthusiastically, "especially since God had to paint it with his left hand."

The father was baffled. "What do you mean, son? His left hand?"

"Well," answered the boy, "my Sunday school teacher said that Jesus was sitting on God's right hand."

# 248

How did Jonah feel when the whale swallowed him? *Down in the mouth.*

# 249

Sunday school teacher: Now, Charlie, what can you tell me about Goliath?

Charlie: Goliath was the man David rocked to sleep.

## 250

The Sunday school teacher had just finished the lesson. She had taught the portion of the Bible that told of how Lot's wife looked back and turned into a pillar of salt.

Jeremy raised his hand. "My mommy looked back once when she was driving, and she turned into a telephone pole!"

## 251

A mother was preparing pancakes for her sons, Jack and Chris. The boys began to argue over who would get the first pancake. Their mother saw the opportunity for a moral lesson. "If Jesus were sitting here, He would say, 'Let My brother have the first pancake; I can wait.'"

Jack turned to his younger brother and said, "Chris, you be Jesus!"

## 252

Why didn't Noah fish very often?
*He only had two worms.*

## 253

A minister was visiting the home of a family in his congregation. Their little son ran in, holding a mouse by the tail.

"Don't worry, Mom, it's dead," he reported. "We chased him, then hit him until. . ."

Just then he caught sight of the minister. He lowered his voice and eyes and finished, ". . .until God called him home."

## 254

A little boy came home with his parents from church one Sunday. He seemed a bit down, so his mother asked him if something happened in Sunday school class that he would like to talk about.

He told his mother, "We were singing songs, and the teacher made us sing about a poor bear named Gladly that needed glasses, and I just can't stop thinking about him. She said he was cross-eyed, and I feel bad for him."

The mother couldn't understand why the teacher would teach such a song in Sunday school, so she decided to call her. To the mother's amazement, the teacher said she only taught hymns that morning.

Then the teacher began laughing out loud and said to the mother, "I know what Jeffrey's talking about! We learned the hymn 'Gladly the Cross I'd Bear.'"

## 255

A man was lying on the grass and looking up at the sky. As he watched the clouds drift by, he asked, "God, how long is a million years?"

God answered, "To Me, a million years is as a minute."

The man asked, "God, how much is a million dollars?"

God answered, "To Me, a million dollars is as a penny."

The man then asked, "God, can I have a penny?"

God answered, "In a minute."

## 256

One cold winter day, a boy was standing outside a shoe store, praying to God for some socks or some shoes. Just then a lady walked up to him and said, "Is there something that I can help you with?"

He looked down at his feet and said, "Well, I would like some shoes."

She grabbed his hand and took him into the shoe store. She asked for a dozen pairs of socks and a pair of shoes. They sat down, and the clerk put a pair of socks and shoes on the boy.

As the woman got up to leave, the boy thanked her. She told him that if he ever needed anything else, to not to be afraid to ask.

He looked at her and asked, "Are you God's wife?"

## 257

A nurse on the pediatric ward, before listening to the children's chests, would fit the stethoscope into their ears and let them listen to their own hearts. Their eyes would always light up with awe.

"Listen," she said to little four-year-old Seth, "Do you hear it? What do you suppose that is?"

He listened to the strange tap-tap-tapping deep in his chest. Then his eyes lit up, and he exclaimed, "Is that Jesus knocking?"

## 258

A little boy in Sunday school was asked what commandment he would break if he stayed home from Sunday school. He replied, "The fourth one: Keep the Sabbath Day holy."

Then he was asked what commandment he would break if he took his friend's bicycle. He replied, "The eighth: Do not steal."

Then he was asked what commandment he would break if he pulled his dog's tail. He hesitated, then said, "I don't know the number, but it goes like this: 'What God has joined together, let no man pull apart.'"

## 259

A young soldier was on guard duty one night. He did his best to stay awake, but he soon drifted off. He suddenly woke up and found his superior standing next to him.

Knowing the penalty for falling asleep while on duty, the soldier lowered his head once more and said, "A–a–a–men."

## 260

The Sunday school lesson was about the prodigal son. Toward the end of the lesson, the teacher asked, "What happened when the prodigal son returned?"

"His father went out to meet him and hurt himself," said Ricky.

"Hurt himself? No, the Bible doesn't tell us he hurt himself," corrected the teacher.

"Oh, yes, it does," replied Ricky. "It says that his father ran to meet him and fell on his neck."

## 261

What was the vehicle of choice among the apostles? *A Honda. . .because they were all in one Accord.*

## 262

A minister told his congregation, "Next week I plan to preach about the sin of lying. To prepare you for my sermon, I want you all to read Mark 17."

The following Sunday, the minister asked all those who had read Mark 17, as requested, to raise their hands. Most of the congregation raised their hands. The minister smiled and said, "Mark has only sixteen chapters. I will now proceed with my sermon on the sin of lying."

## 263

A four-year-old boy was asked to pray before dinner. The family members bowed their heads. He began his prayer, thanking God for all his friends and family members. Then he began to thank God for the food. He gave thanks for the chicken, the mashed potatoes, the fruit salad, and even the milk. Then he paused, and everyone waited.

After a long silence, the little boy opened one eye, looked at his mother, and asked, "If I thank God for the broccoli, won't He know that I'm lying?"

## 264

A businessman needed a large sum of money to clinch an important deal. He went to church to pray for the money. By chance he knelt next to a man who was praying for one hundred dollars to pay an urgent debt.

The businessman took out his wallet and gave one hundred dollars to the other man. Overjoyed, the man got up and left the church.

The businessman then closed his eyes and prayed, "Lord, now that I have Your undivided attention. . ."

## 265

The Sunday school teacher was explaining the story of Elijah and the false prophets of Baal. She explained how Elijah built the altar, cut the bull into pieces, and laid those pieces and wood upon the altar.

Then Elijah commanded the people of God to fill four barrels of water and pour it the altar. He had them do this three times.

"Can anyone tell me why Elijah would ask the people to pour water over the bull on the altar?" asked the teacher.

A little girl excitedly answered, "To make the gravy!"

## 266

It was Palm Sunday, and Mary's four-year-old son stayed home from church with his father, because he was sick.

When his siblings returned home carrying palm branches, the little boy asked what the branches were for.

His mother explained, "People held them over Jesus' head as He walked by."

"I can't believe it," the boy said. "I miss one Sunday, and Jesus shows up!"

## 267

A nearsighted minister glanced at the note that Mrs. Edwards had sent to him by an usher.

The note read: "Phil Edwards having gone to sea, his wife desires the prayers of the congregation for his safety."

The minister failed to observe the punctuation, however, and surprised the congregation when he read aloud, "Phil Edwards, having gone to see his wife, desires the prayers of the congregation for his safety."

## 268

A woman and her five-year-old son were headed to McDonald's. On the way, they passed a car accident.

As was their habit when seeing an accident, they prayed for whoever was involved.

After the mother prayed, she asked her son if he would, too. "Please, God," he prayed, "don't let those cars be blocking the entrance to McDonald's."

## 269

At a church dinner, there was a pile of apples on one end of a table with a sign that read, TAKE ONLY ONE APPLE, PLEASE. GOD IS WATCHING.

On the other end of the table was a pile of cookies where a youth had placed a sign saying, TAKE ALL THE COOKIES YOU WANT. GOD IS WATCHING THE APPLES.

## 270

Who was the greatest financier in the Bible?
*Noah; he was floating his stock while everyone else was in liquidation.*

## 271

At Sunday school, Mr. Duncan told his students that God created everything, including human beings. Freddy seemed especially intent when Mr. Duncan explained that Eve was created out of one of Adam's ribs.

Later in the week, his mother noticed him lying on the floor and asked, "Freddy, what is the matter?"

Freddy responded, "I have a pain in my side. I think I'm gonna have a wife."

## 272

The Sunday school teacher was telling his class the story of the prodigal son. Attempting to emphasize the bitterness of the elder brother, he laid stress on that part of the parable.

After describing the rejoicing of the household over the return of the wayward son, the teacher spoke of one who failed to share in the joyful spirit. "Can anyone tell me who this was?" he asked the class.

"I know! I know!" a young girl responded. "It was the fattened calf."

## 273

Which Bible character had no parents?
*Joshua. He was the son of Nun.*

## 274

A father was approached by his small son, who told him proudly, "I know what the Bible means!"

His father smiled and replied, "What do you mean, you know what the Bible means?"

The son replied, "B-Basic, I-Instructions, B-Before, L-Leaving, E-Earth."

## 275

A Sunday school teacher was reading a Bible story to her class. "The man named Lot was warned to take his wife and flee out of the city, but his wife looked back and turned to salt."

A little boy softly asked, "What happened to the flea?"

## 276

Who was the greatest female financier in the Bible? *Pharaoh's daughter; she went down to the bank of the Nile and drew out a little prophet.*

## 277

A minister got up on Sunday and announced to his congregation, "I have good news and bad news. The good news is, we have enough money to pay for our new building program. The bad news is, it's still out there in your pockets."

## 278

A Sunday school teacher asked her little students, as they were on the way to the church service, "And why should we be quiet in church?"

A little girl replied, "Because people are sleeping."

## 279

A child was watching his mother delete e-mail messages from her in-box.

"This reminds me of the Lord's Prayer," the child said.

"What do you mean?" asked the mother.

"Oh, you know. That part that says, 'Deliver us from e-mail.'"

## 280

When is the first tennis match mentioned in the Bible?
*When Joseph served in Pharaoh's court.*

## 281

Two old friends met one day after many years. The one who had attended college was now quite successful. The other had not attended college and never had much ambition.

The successful one said, "How has everything been going with you?"

"Well, one day, I closed my eyes, opened my Bible, and pointed. When I opened my eyes, I read the word *oil*. So I invested in oil, and the wells flowed. Then another day I dropped my finger on another word and it was *gold*. So I invested in gold, and those mines really produced. Now I have millions of dollars."

The successful friend was so impressed that he ran home, grabbed his Bible, closed his eyes, flipped it open, and dropped his finger on a page. He opened his eyes and read the words *Chapter Eleven*.

# 282

A painter was hired to paint the exterior of a church. His practice was to thin the paint so that he could make a larger profit.

As he was painting the church, torrential rain began to fall, and it washed all of the paint off. As quickly as the rain began, it ended, and the sun came out. The painter gazed skyward, and a voice from above said, "Repaint, and go and thin no more."

# 283

What was Noah's profession?
*He was an ark-itect.*

# 284

Was Noah the first one out of the ark?
*No; he came forth out of the ark.*

# 285

What did Noah say as he was loading the ark?
*"Now I herd everything."*

## 286

Sunday school teacher: What happened to Tyre?
Student: The Lord punctured it.

## 287

A little boy was praying at bedtime.
"I can't hear you," whispered his mother.
"I'm not talking to you," the boy whispered back.

## 288

A young boy had been begging his father for a new watch. His father, getting frustrated, finally demanded, "I don't want to hear about your wanting a watch again."

At family devotions that evening, each family member was asked to share a Bible verse. The boy read Mark 13:37: "And what I say unto you I say unto all, Watch."

## 289

On the first night of his grandmother's visit, a small boy was saying his prayers.

"Please Lord," he shouted, "send me a bicycle, a tool chest, a. . ."

"Why are you praying so loud?" his older brother interrupted. "God isn't deaf."

"I know He isn't," replied the boy. "But Grandma is."

## 290

Answering the phone, the minister was surprised to hear the caller introduce herself as an IRS auditor.

"But we do not pay taxes," the minister said.

"It isn't you, sir, it's a member of your congregation, Neil Smythe. He indicates on his tax return that he gave a donation of fifteen thousand dollars to the church last year. Is this true?"

The minister smiled broadly. "The check hasn't arrived yet, but I'm sure I'll have it after I remind Neil."

## 291

One Sunday morning, a man was pulled over by a motorcycle cop for speeding. As the officer asked the driver for his license and registration, passing motorists would slow down, then honk and wave.

After about the twelfth driver passed by, honking and waving, the officer asked the speeder what was going on. The driver told him, "I am the minister at the church a mile down the road. That's where I was going when you stopped me. The members of my congregation recognized me."

The officer smiled and tore up the ticket. "I think you've paid your debt to society," he proclaimed.

## 292

The front door of Todd's home warped, causing the door to jam on occasion. To pry it open, the family kept a hatchet handy.

One day the doorbell rang. Todd peeked out through the curtains and then shouted in a voice that could be heard through the door, "Quick, Kevin, it's the pastor. Get the hatchet!"

# EDUCATION

## 293

A schoolteacher had injured his back and had to wear a plaster cast around the upper part of his body. It was not noticeable at all under his shirt.

On the first day of school, he discovered that many of his students were unruly and disrespectful. He confidently walked to the window and opened it. He then sat at his desk and began looking at his notes. When a strong breeze made his tie flap, he took the stapler and stapled the tie to his chest.

He had no trouble with discipline that year.

## 294

Principal: This is the fourth time you've been in my office this week. What do you have to say for yourself?
Sam: I'm so glad today is Friday!

## 295

Jeanne: Mom, I got a hundred in school today!
Mom: Good job! What did you get a hundred in?
Jeanne: In two things. I got a forty in math and a sixty in spelling.

## 296

Jim: Teacher, would you be mad at somebody for something they didn't do?
Teacher: No, of course not.
Jim: Good. I didn't do my homework.

## 297

Teacher: Cathy, what would you do if you were being chased by a man-eating tiger?
Cathy: Nothing. I'm a girl.

## 298

What two letters of the alphabet contain nothing?
*M.T.*

## 299

What is it that we have in December that we don't have in any other month?
*The letter* D.

## 300

What is the longest word in the English language?
*Smiles. There's a mile between the Ss.*

## 301

What word starts with *E* and has only one letter in it?
*Envelope.*

## 302

What makes math such hard work?
*All those numbers you have to carry.*

## 303

The English professor at school emphasized, over and over again, the importance of developing an extensive vocabulary.

"You have my assurance," he told the class, "that if you repeat a word eight or ten times, it will be yours for life."

In the back row, an attractive young woman sighed and, closing her eyes, whispered softly to herself, "Steve, Steve, Steve. . ."

## 304

Father: How did you do on your tests today?
Daughter: Okay, but on one I was like Washington and Lincoln.
Father: What do you mean?
Daughter: I went down in history.

## 305

Teacher: The law of gravity explains why we stay on the ground.
Chloe: How did we stay on the ground before the law was passed?

## 306

Dad: Could you explain the *D* and *F* on your report card?
Son: No problem. It stands for "Doing Fine."

## 307

What did one math book say to the other?
*"Man, I got a lot of problems!"*

## 308

Charlie: Hey, Mom, tomorrow there's a small PTA meeting.
Mom: What do you mean by "small"?
Charlie: Well, it's just you, me, and the principal.

## 309

Son: Great news, Dad!
Dad: What's the great news?
Son: You don't have to buy me any new books next year. I'm taking all of the same courses again.

## 310

Science teacher: What is the difference between electricity and lightning?
Student: We don't have to pay for lightning.

## 311

I'm reading an incredibly interesting book about antigravity. I just can't put it down.

## 312

"Just to establish some parameters," said the professor, "Mr. Nelson, what is the opposite of joy?"

"Sadness," said the student.

"And the opposite of depression, Ms. Brady?"

"Elation."

"And you, Mr. Jackson, how about the opposite of woe?"

"I believe that would be giddyap."

## 313

"Tell me," the teacher asked her students, "do you know what the word *can't* is short for?"

"Yes," said little Lucy. "It's short for *cannot.*"

"Very good. And what about *don't?*"

Little Matt's hand shot up. "That," he said with authority, "is short for *doughnut.*"

## 314

A little boy, who was doing his homework one evening, turned to his father and said, "Dad, where would I find the Andes?"

"Don't ask me," said the father. "Ask your mother. She puts everything away in this house."

## 315

What kind of food do math teachers eat?
*Square meals.*

## 316

Why did the amoeba flunk the math test?
*Because it multiplied by dividing.*

## 317

At the beginning of math class, the teacher asked, "Timmy, what are 3 and 6 and 27 and 45?"

Timmy quickly answered, "NBC, CBS, ESPN, and the Cartoon Network!"

## 318

Three friends were walking home from school. "What should we do this afternoon?" said the first.

"I know," said the second, "let's flip a coin. If it comes down heads, let's go skating, and if it comes down tails, let's go swimming."

"And if it comes down on its edge," said the third, "let's stay in and do our homework!"

## 319

Which two words have the most letters in them?
*Post office.*

## 320

What state is round on both sides but high in the middle?
*Ohio.*

## 321

What's a teacher's favorite candy?
*Chalk-olate.*

## 322

Did you hear about the delivery van loaded with thesauruses that crashed into a taxi?
*Witnesses were astounded, shocked, taken aback, surprised, startled, dumbfounded, thunderstruck, caught unawares. . . .*

## 323

What is the best state to get school supplies?
*Pencil-vania.*

## 324

Why is the library the tallest room in the school?
*It has the most stories.*

## 325

What can spell every word in every language?
*An echo.*

## 326

A mother said, "Son, it's time to get up and go to school."

"Mom," her son replied, "nobody at school likes me—the students don't, the teachers don't, the bus drivers don't. . . . I don't want to go to school!"

His mom firmly said, "Son, you must go to school. You are healthy, you have a lot to learn, and you are a leader. . .and besides, you are the principal!"

## 327

Where does Thursday come before Wednesday?
*In the dictionary.*

## 328

Why is a bad joke like a broken pencil?
*It has no point.*

## 329

What do math teachers like to eat with their coffee?
*A slice of pi.*

## 330

Who invented fractions?
*Henry the 1/8th.*

## 331

Every year, the teacher sent a note home with each child that read, "Dear Parents, if you promise not to believe everything your child says happens at school, I'll promise not to believe everything he or she says happens at home."

## 332

The kindergarten class had settled down to its coloring books. Jonathon raised his hand and said, "Miss Franklin, I ain't got no crayons."

"Jonathon," Miss Franklin said, "you mean, 'I don't have any crayons. You don't have any crayons. We don't have any crayons. They don't have any crayons.'"

"Well," said Jonathon, "what happened to all the crayons?"

## 333

A philosophy professor gave a one-question final exam. He picked up his chair, plopped it on his desk, and wrote on the board: "Using everything we have learned this semester, prove that this chair does not exist."

The students began furiously writing their answers. However, one member of the class finished in less than a minute. He turned his paper in and left the room.

Weeks later when the grades were posted, the rest of the class wondered how he could have gotten an A when he had barely written anything at all.

His answer consisted of two words: "What chair?"

## 334

Teacher: Correct this sentence: "It was me who broke the window."
Joey: It wasn't me who broke the window!

## 335

Teacher: What is the plural of *mouse*?
Student: Mice.
Teacher: Good. Now, what's the plural of *baby*?
Student: Twins!

## 336

The school board determined that speech and debate would be removed from the course schedule; there was no argument.

## 337

Father: Tim, I think the reason you're getting such bad grades is because you spend too much time watching game shows on television.
Son: Dad, could you please phrase that in the form of a question?

## 338

Why can you always tell what Dick and Jane will do next?
*They're so easy to read.*

## 339

Teacher: If I cut a steak in two, then cut the halves in two, what do I get?
Student: Quarters.
Teacher: Very good. And what would I get if I cut it again?
Student: Eighths.
Teacher: Great job! And if I cut it again?
Student: Sixteenths.
Teacher: Wonderful! And again?
Student: Hamburger.

## 340

A teacher had just discussed magnets with her class. At the close of the lesson, she said, "My name begins with *m* and I pick up things. What am I?"

Julia thought for a moment, then answered, "Mom!"

## 341

A kindergarten teacher was having a difficult time putting each child's boots on after a very rainy morning. After some hard tugging, she finally got Barry's on his feet when he said, "These aren't mine."

The frustrated teacher had to pull hard to remove them from the little lad's feet.

She sat down next to him and asked, "So, whose boots are these?"

Barry answered, "They're my brother's, but my mom lets me wear them."

## 342

Teacher: Can anyone give me the name of a liquid that won't freeze?
Sam: Hot water.

## 343

Teacher: Please tell me something important that didn't exist fifty years ago.
Student: Me!

## 344

Why isn't there any difference between a "fat chance" and a "slim chance"?

## 345

An English professor wrote the following words on the blackboard: "Woman without her man is nothing." He then requested that his students punctuate the sentence correctly.

The men wrote: "Woman, without her man, is nothing."

The women wrote: "Woman! Without her, man is nothing."

## 346

Tracy hadn't talked to her grandparents for a while and decided she should call and update them.

"I had a terrible time!" she told them. "First off I got tonsillitis, followed by appendicitis and pneumonia. After that, I got rheumatism, and to top it off they gave me hypodermics and inoculations. I thought I would *never* get through that spelling bee!"

## 347

Father: You have four Ds and a C on your report card!

Son: I know. I think I concentrated too much on the one subject.

## 348

Mrs. Oliver asked her class to write a composition on the subject of baseball. "You have thirty minutes to complete it," she told her class.

Sarah handed in her paper after writing for less than a minute.

"You can't be finished already," said Mrs. Oliver.

"Yes, I am," proclaimed Sarah.

Mrs. Oliver looked at her paper and read: "Game called off on account of rain."

## 349

Mrs. Davis asked her English class, "Can anyone give me a sentence with a direct object?"

Zach raised his hand and said, "Everyone thinks you are the best teacher in the school."

"Why, thank you, Zach," replied Mrs. Davis. "And what is the object?"

"To get the best grade I can," said Zach.

## 350

Teacher: What are the Great Plains?
Student: The 747, Concorde, and F-16.

## 351

Shortly after Christmas vacation, Jasmine came home with a bad report card. Her mother asked her, "What was the trouble?"

Jasmine answered, "Oh, there was no trouble. You know how things are always marked down after the holidays."

## 352

A third-grade class went to an art museum. They were instructed to sit and wait until the guide was ready to begin the tour. Two boys, however, decided to explore on their own. They walked down a hallway and entered a room filled with modern art pieces.

"Quick," said one, "run—before they say we did it!"

## 353

Laugh, and the class laughs with you. But you get detention alone.

## 354

Playing hooky is like a credit card. Fun now, pay later.

## 355

Dad: Why were you expelled from school?
Matt: I used a hose to fill up the swimming pool.
Dad: I didn't know the school had a swimming pool.
Matt: Well, it does now!

## 356

A linguistics professor was lecturing his class one day. "In the English language," he said, "a double negative forms a positive. In other languages, such as Russian, a double negative is still a negative. However, there is no language wherein a double positive can form a negative."

A voice from the back of the room said, "Yeah, right."

## 357

Miss Evans addressed her third-grade class after recess: "Did anyone lose a dollar on the playground?"

"I did, Miss Evans," said Rob. "A dollar bill fell out of my pocket."

"But this was four quarters," said Miss Evans.

"Hmm," replied Rob. "It must have broken when it hit the ground."

## 358

How did you pass the entrance exam for candy-making school?
*It was simple. I fudged it.*

## 359

Jennifer: Are you in the top half of your class?
Laura: No, I'm one of the students who make the top half possible.

## 360

A man was visiting his alma mater. He paused to admire the newly constructed Shakespeare Hall.

"It's marvelous to see a building named for William Shakespeare," he commented to the tour guide.

"Actually," said the guide, "it's named for Stephen Shakespeare. No relation."

"Oh, was Stephen Shakespeare a writer, also?" the visitor asked.

"Well, yes," said his guide. "He wrote the check."

## 361

What starts with *T*, ends with *T*, and is full of *T*?
*Teapot.*

## 362

Lizzie's parents received a note from her first-grade teacher.

"Lizzie is a wonderful student," the teacher wrote, "but when we have coloring projects, she draws everything in gray. Flowers, people, the sky, buildings, cars, grass—everything is gray. This is highly unusual for a first-grade student. Can you think of a possible explanation? I think it would be in her best interest for us to assist her in working through whatever problem she may have."

That night, Lizzie's parents sat down with her and asked her why everything she drew was in gray. "Why have you chosen that as your special color?" they asked her.

"Well," she began, "I didn't want to tell you. But a couple of weeks ago I lost my new box of crayons. The only one I have left is the gray one I found in the pocket of my backpack."

## 363

What would life be like if there were no hypothetical questions?

# ELECTRONICS
# AND
# MECHANISMS

## 364

What did the big hand on the clock say to the little hand?
*"I'll be around in an hour."*

## 365

Computer salesperson: This computer will do half your work for you.
Customer: Then I'll take two!

## 366

A mountaineer and his son went to the city for the first time. In one of the buildings, the man saw a set of doors open, an old woman enter, and the doors close. Soon the doors opened again, and a young woman stepped out.

The man turned to his son and said, "You stay here. I'm going for your mother to run her through that machine."

## 367

What do videos do on their days off?
*They unwind.*

## 368

A kind woman watched a small boy as he tried to reach the doorbell of a house.

Thinking she should help, she walked up to the doorbell and rang it for him.

"Okay, what now?" the woman asked the boy.

"Run like crazy," he answered. "That's what I'm gonna do!"

## 369

Father to teenage daughter: Did I hear the clock strike two as you came in last night?

Daughter: Oh, it started to strike eleven, but I stopped it so that it wouldn't wake you up.

## 370

Which way did the programmer go?
*He went data way.*

## 371

Why was the computer so tired when it got home from the office?
*Because it had a hard drive.*

## 372

What kind of cola do keyboards like?
*Tab.*

## 373

Tech Support: I need you to right-click.
Customer: Okay.
Tech Support: Did you get a pop-up menu?
Customer: No.
Tech Support: Okay. Right-click again. Do you see a pop-up menu?
Customer: No.
Tech Support: Okay, sir. Can you tell me what you have done up until this point?
Customer: Sure, you told me to write "click" and I wrote "click."

## 374

When you read a message on your computer that says, THE APPLICATION CAUSED AN ERROR. CHOOSE IGNORE OR CLOSE, it means, IT DOESN'T MAKE ANY DIFFERENCE; YOU'RE NEVER GOING TO SEE YOUR WORK AGAIN.

## 375

How can you tell a good computer programmer from a bad computer programmer?
*The good one always comes through when the chips are down.*

## 376

Remember when. . .
- . . .an application was for employment?
- . . .a CD was a bank account?
- . . .a program was a show on television?
- . . .a web was a spider's home?
- . . .a hard drive was a long car ride?
- . . .memory was something you lost as you got older?
- . . .a keyboard was a piano?
- . . .a virus was the flu?

## 377

Why don't computers eat anything?
*They don't like what's on their menus.*

## 378

How do you catch a runaway computer?
*With an Internet.*

## 379

Why did the man turn on his computer on a hot day?
*He wanted to open the Windows.*

## 380

Why couldn't the girl type on her computer?
*She lost her keys.*

## 381

What's the first sign that a computer is getting old?
*It has memory problems.*

## 382

Why shouldn't you take your computer into rush-hour traffic?
*Because it might crash.*

## 383

Back in the 1800s the Tates Watch Company of Massachusetts wanted to expand their product line, and since they already made the cases for pocket watches, they decided to market compasses for the pioneers traveling west. Although their watches were of the finest quality, their compasses were so bad that people were continually getting lost.

This, of course, is the origin of the expression, "He who has a Tates is lost!"

## 384

What's the difference between a red light and a green light?
*The color, silly.*

## 385

A frustrated father vented, "When I was a teenager and got in trouble, I was sent to my room without supper. But my son has his own color television, telephone, computer, and CD player in his room."

"So what do you do to him?" asked his friend.

"I send him to *my* room!" exclaimed the father.

## 386

What do you call a watch worn on a belt?
*A waist of time.*

## 387

The new housekeeper answered the telephone and replied, "Yes, you are correct."

Again the phone rang and the housekeeper answered it. "Yes, ma'am, it certainly is!"

"Who was that?" asked the owner of the house.

"I really don't know," she replied. "Some woman kept saying, 'It's a long-distance call from Canada,' and I said, 'It certainly is!'"

## 388

A couple owned a grandfather clock that struck each hour. It began to malfunction one day, striking five at ten o'clock, striking nine at two o'clock, and so on.

That night at eleven o'clock, it struck fourteen.

The woman jumped up and shook her husband, saying, "Get up, dear! It's later than it's ever been before!"

## 389

Two kids went into their parents' bathroom and noticed the scale in the corner.

"Whatever you do," said one youngster to the other, "don't step on it!"

"Why not?" asked the sibling.

"Because every time Mom does, she lets out an awful loud scream!"

## 390

A computer technician was called to a small business to repair a computer. He wasn't able to find a close parking spot, so he left his car in a No Parking zone and placed a note on his windshield saying, "James Bauer, computer technician, working inside the building."

He completed his work within thirty minutes and returned to his car to find a ticket with a note that read, "Peter Westin, police officer, working outside the building."

# FAMILY
# MATTERS

## 391

Lizzie: Mommy, Zach broke my baby doll.
Mommy: I'm sorry, sweetheart. How did it happen?
Lizzie: I hit him over the head with it.

## 392

Mother: Tommy, why did you kick your little sister in the stomach?
Tommy: I couldn't help it. She turned around too quick.

## 393

Mother: Why are you crying?
Mark: Dad hit his hand with a hammer.
Mother: I'm surprised you're not laughing.
Mark: I did.

## 394

Elizabeth: My mom has the worst memory.
Melissa: She forgets everything?
Elizabeth: No, she remembers everything.

### 395

Mother: Kids, what are you arguing about?
David: Oh, there isn't any argument. Lisa thinks I'm not going to give her half of my candy, and I think the same thing.

### 396

Gabe: Why are you down?
Mike: My sister said she wouldn't talk to me for two weeks.
Gabe: Why should that upset you?
Mike: Today's the last day.

### 397

Petey came home from school with another black eye. "Have you been fighting again?" his mother asked him.

"I'm sorry, Mom," he replied.

"I told you the next time you lost your temper, you should count to ten."

"I did," said Petey. "But Jimmy's mom told him to only count to five, so he hit me first."

## 398

A man was purchasing a fountain pen. "I suppose this is to be a surprise, sir?" asked the clerk.

"Oh, yes it is," replied the man. "It's my son's birthday, and he asked for a new car."

## 399

It is truly said that children brighten a home—they never turn off the lights.

## 400

A young child walked up to her mother and stared at her hair. As her mother scrubbed on the dishes, the girl cleared her throat and asked, "Why do you have some gray hairs?"

The mother paused and looked at her daughter. "Every time you disobey, I get a strand of gray hair."

The mother returned to her task of washing dishes. The little girl stood there thinking. She cleared her throat again. "Mom?" she said.

"Yes?" her mother answered.

"Why is Grandma's hair all gray?"

# 401

A little girl asked her mother, "Can I go outside and play with the boys?"

Her mother replied, "No, you can't play with the boys; they're too rough."

The little girl thought about it for a few moments and then asked, "If I can find a smooth one, can I play with him?"

# 402

A three-year-old had been told several times to get ready for bed. The last time his mom told him, she was very insistent. His response was, "Yes, sir!"

Correcting him, she said, "You would say, 'yes, sir,' to a man. I am a lady, and you would say 'yes, ma'am,' to a lady."

To quiz him on this lesson, she then asked him, "What would you say to Daddy?"

"Yes, sir!" came the reply.

"Then what would you say to Mama?"

"Yes, ma'am!" he proudly answered.

"Good job! Now, what would you say to Grandma?"

He lit up and said, "Can I have a cookie?"

## 403

A father sent his boy to bed. Five minutes later, he heard, "D–a–a–a–d!"

"What?" he called back.

"I'm thirsty. Can you bring a drink of water?"

"No. You had your chance. Lights out."

Five minutes later, he again heard, "D–a–a–a–d!"

"What?"

"I'm thirsty. Can I have a drink of water?"

"I told you no! If you ask again, I'll have to spank you!"

Five minutes later, came, "D–a–a–a–d!"

*"What!"*

"When you come in to spank me, can you bring a drink of water?"

## 404

When the Smith family moved into their new house, a visiting grandparent asked five-year-old Tommy how he liked the new place.

"It's great," he said. "I have my own room, Alex has his own room, and Jamie has her own room. But poor Mom is still in with Dad."

## 405

Hearing a scream from the playroom, the mother rushed in and found her infant son pulling the hair of his four-year-old sister. After separating them, the mother said to her daughter, "Don't be upset with your brother, honey. He didn't know he was hurting you." No sooner had the mother returned to her chores than she heard more screaming. This time she rushed in and found the baby crying. "Now what happened?" she asked.

"Nothing," said the girl, "except that now he knows."

## 406

What is the opposite of minimum?
*Minidad.*

## 407

It was local election time, and the candidate was visiting all the houses in his area. At one house, a small boy answered the door.

"Tell me, young man," said the politician, "is your Mommy in the Republican Party or the Democratic Party?"

"Neither," said the child. "She's in the bathroom."

## 408

When do mothers have baby boys?
*On son days.*

## 409

Mom: A rabbit's house is called a warren, alligators have nests, and foxes live in dens. What do you call your room?
Son: A mess.

## 410

Who is bigger—Mr. Bigger or Mr. Bigger's baby?
*Mr. Bigger's baby is a little Bigger.*

## 411

A mother saw her young son come through the door with filthy hands. She stopped him and said, "My goodness, what would you say if I came in the house with hands like that?"

Her son looked at her and answered, "I think I'd be too polite to mention it."

## 412

After being punished for losing his temper, a little boy asked his mother, "Can you explain to me the difference between my foul temper and your worn nerves?"

## 413

A mother came inside after gardening and found a big hole in the middle of the pie she had made earlier that morning. She found a gooey spoon lying in the sink and crumbs all over the floor.

She went to find her son. "David," she said, "you promised me that you wouldn't touch the pie I made. And I promised you that if you did touch the pie, I would spank you."

A look of relief came over David. "Now that I've broken my promise," he said, "I think it would be all right for you to break yours, too."

## 414

A father was showing pictures of his wedding day to his son. "Is that when Mommy came to work for us?" the boy asked.

## 415

Ted: You seem unhappy.
Roger: Yeah, I am. Living with my mother-in-law has been stressful. It's been hard on both me and my wife.
Ted: Well, if it gets really bad, you could just ask her to move out.
Roger: We can't. It's her house.

## 416

A man and his wife attended a dinner party at the home of their friends. Near the end of the meal, the wife reprimanded her husband.

"That's the third time you've gone for dessert," she scolded. "The hostess must think you're an absolute pig."

"I don't think so," he said. "I've been telling her it's for you."

## 417

My teenage daughter thinks I'm too nosy. At least that's what she keeps writing in her diary.

# Finances

## 418

Husband: What do you mean, our financial situation is fluid?
Wife: We're going down the drain.

## 419

Husband: The bank returned your check.
Wife: Good, now I can use it for something else.

## 420

Stan: Remember last year when I was broke and you helped me and I said I'd never forget you?
Fred: Yes, I remember.
Stan: Well, I'm broke again.

## 421

A little boy showed his father a ten-dollar bill he had found in the street.

"Are you sure it was lost?" asked his father.

"Yes," answered the boy. "I saw the man looking for it."

## 422

If money grew on trees, where would you keep it?
*In a branch bank.*

## 423

Here's a suggestion for parents who naturally become worried when their youngsters are away from home, either at camp or college, and neglect to write.

Send the child your usual letter and add this postscript: "Hope you can use the fifty dollars I am enclosing."

## 424

A big-city counterfeiter thought the best place to pass off his phony eighteen-dollar bills would be in a small country town. So, he went off in search of one.

When he found a town that he thought might work, the counterfeiter entered a store and handed one of the bogus bills to the cashier.

"Can I have change for this, please?" he asked.

The store clerk looked at the eighteen-dollar bill, then smiled and replied, "Sure, mister. Would you like two nines or three sixes?"

## 425

When you borrow money, borrow it from a pessimist. He won't expect you to pay him back.

## 426

Joan and her neighbor were talking about their daughters. Rebekah said, "My daughter is at the university. She's very bright, you know. Every time we get a letter from her, we have to go to the dictionary."

Her neighbor said, "You are so fortunate. Every time we hear from our daughter, we have to go to the bank."

## 427

A woman who ran to the mall for a quick errand lost her purse, but an honest teenage boy returned it to her.

The woman looked inside her purse and remarked, "That's really odd. Earlier I had a twenty-dollar bill inside, but now it's gone. Instead, I see four fives."

"Well," the boy explained, "the last time I found a lady's purse, she didn't have change for a reward."

## 428

Tired of having to balance his wife Dot's checkbook, Dave made a deal with her; he would only look at it after she had spent a few hours trying to get it into shape. Only then would he lend his expertise.

The following night, after spending hours poring over the figures, Dot said, "There! I did it! I made it balance!"

Dave was impressed and came over to take a look. "Let's see. . .mortgage, seven hundred dollars; electricity, sixty-four dollars and twelve cents; telephone, thirty-eight dollars and seventy-three cents. . ." His brow wrinkled as he read the last entry. "It says here ESP, six hundred and forty-four dollars. What is that?"

"Oh," she said, "that means 'Error Some Place.'"

## 429

A spokesperson for the U.S. Mint announced that a new fifty-cent piece was being issued to honor two great American patriots. On one side of the coin would be Teddy Roosevelt and on the other side, Nathan Hale.

Asked why two people were going to be on the same coin, the spokesman replied, "Now, when you toss a coin, you can simply call 'Teds' or 'Hales.'"

## 430

What has a head and a tail but no body?
*A coin.*

## 431

Where is the safest place to keep money in America?
*The Outer Banks.*

## 432

A teenager was telling her father all about her new boyfriend.

"He sounds very nice," said her father. "Does he have any money?"

"You men are all alike," she said. "He asked the same thing about you."

## 433

"I see our neighbors have returned our grill," the wife commented. "They've had it for eight months, and I was afraid that in their move, they'd take it with them by mistake."

"That was *our* grill?" shouted her husband. "I just paid twenty dollars for it at their yard sale!"

# Food

# 434

How many items can you put into an empty grocery bag?
*One. After that, the bag isn't empty anymore.*

# 435

What is the smallest room in the world?
*The mushroom.*

# 436

What has no teeth, no mouth, but does have eyes and lives in the ground?
*A potato.*

# 437

What's more useful after it's broken?
*An egg.*

# 438

Diner: Is there any stew on the menu?
Waiter: There was, but I wiped it off.

## 439

Diner: Waiter! You have your finger on my steak!
Waiter: Well, I don't want it to fall on the floor again.

## 440

Waitress: Have I kept you waiting long?
Customer: No, but did you know that there are 3,296 squares on the ceiling?

## 441

When the mother returned from the grocery store, her small son pulled out the box of animal crackers he had begged for. Then he spread the animal-shaped crackers all over the kitchen counter.

"What are you doing?" his mom asked.

"The box says you can't eat them if the seal is broken," the boy explained. "I'm looking for the seal."

## 442

Why couldn't the coffee bean go out to play?
*He was grounded.*

## 443

A new bride cooked her first meal for her husband. "My mother taught me to cook, and I can cook two things well—apple pie and meatloaf."

The husband took a bite of his supper and asked, "And which one is this?"

## 444

What kind of dance does a butcher go to?
*A meatball.*

## 445

What did baby corn say to mama corn?
*"Where's Popcorn?"*

## 446

While eating in an expensive restaurant, a patron overhead the gentleman at the next table ask the waitress to pack the leftovers for their dog. The gentleman's young son then exclaimed, "Whoopee! We're going to get a dog!"

## 447

Waiter: And how did you find your steak, sir?
Customer: Well, I just pushed aside a bean and there
　　it was!

## 448

"Inflation is creeping up," a young man said to his friend. "Yesterday I ordered a twenty-five-dollar steak in a restaurant and told them to put it on my credit card—and it fit."

## 449

What did the soda say to the bottle opener?
*"Hey, can you help me find my pop?"*

## 450

"I thought you were going to count calories," Lois gently reminded her friend Karla as she consumed her second milkshake.

　　"Oh, I am," said Karla. "So far today, I'm at 5,760."

## 451

Why was the mushroom the hit of the party?
*He was a fungi.*

## 452

One morning a little boy proudly surprised his grandmother with a cup of coffee he had made himself. He anxiously waited to hear the verdict on the quality of the coffee. The grandmother had never in her life had such a bad cup of coffee, and as she forced down the last sip, she noticed three of those little green army guys in the bottom of the cup.

She asked, "Honey, why would three little green army guys be in the bottom of my cup?"

Her grandson replied, "You know, Grammy, it's just like on television. 'The best part of waking up is soldiers in your cup.'"

## 453

Why did the other vegetables like the corn?
*He was always willing to lend an ear.*

## 454

What's small, round, and blue?
*A cranberry holding its breath.*

## 455

What kind of beans won't grow in a garden?
*Jelly beans.*

## 456

Why shouldn't you gossip in fields?
*Because corn has ears, potatoes have eyes, and beanstalk.*

## 457

Why don't eggs tell jokes?
*They would crack each other up.*

## 458

Would Little Miss Muffet share her curds?
*No whey.*

## 459

A customer was continually bothering the waiter in a restaurant. First, he asked that the air-conditioning be turned up because he was too hot; then he asked that it be turned down because he was too cold. That continued for about half an hour.

The waiter was very patient, walking back and forth and never once getting angry. Finally, a second customer asked why they just didn't ask the man to leave.

"Oh, I don't mind," said the waiter calmly. "We don't even have an air-conditioner."

# HiSTORY

## 460

What fruits are mentioned the most in history?
*Dates.*

## 461

How did Betsy Ross like her work?
*Sew, sew.*

## 462

Where was the Declaration of Independence signed?
*On the bottom.*

## 463

What was the colonists' favorite tea?
*Liberty.*

## 464

When Betsy Ross washed the flag, why did she use starch?
*She wanted a permanent wave.*

## 465

How did Benjamin Franklin feel when he discovered electricity?
*Shocked.*

## 466

When do knights arrive for sporting events?
*Joust in time.*

## 467

Why didn't George Washington need a bed?
*He would not lie.*

## 468

Did you hear about the King Arthur stamp?
*It's for over-knight delivery.*

## 469

What did Paul Revere say at the end of his famous ride?
*"Whoa!"*

# 470

What didn't King Arthur get served at the Round Table?
*A square meal.*

# 471

Which vegetable was not permitted on the Mayflower?
*The leek.*

# 472

If George Washington went to Washington wearing a white winter coat while his wife waited in Wilmington, how many *W*s are there in all?
*None. There are no Ws in the word all.*

# 473

Why were the Middle Ages also called the Dark Ages?
*Because there were so many knights.*

# 474

Daniel Webster was far from home when night came. Making his way through the darkness, he came upon a farmhouse and knocked on the door. After several minutes, the farmer opened the upstairs window and asked, "What do you want?"

"I wish to spend the night here," replied Webster.

"Fine. Spend the night there," said the farmer, and he closed the window.

# 475

What was Camelot?
*A place where people parked their camels.*

# 476

"My teacher reminds me of history. She's always repeating herself."

# 477

Who invented King Arthur's Round Table?
*Sir Cumference.*

## 478

Which hero of the Revolutionary War slept with his shoes on?
*Paul Revere's horse.*

## 479

Teacher: What happened in 1809?
Eddie: Abraham Lincoln was born.
Teacher: Right. Now, what happened in 1812?
Eddie: He turned three years old.

## 480

What do you call a knight who just lost a fencing match?
*A sword loser.*

## 481

History teacher: Who succeeded the first president of the U.S.?
Student: The second one.

## 482

Where were the kings and queens of England crowned?
*On their heads.*

# Law and Order

## 483

Chris: Uh-oh. I just made an illegal left turn.
Mike: That's okay. The police car behind you did the same thing.

## 484

Judge: The last time I saw you, I told you I didn't want to ever see you again.
Defendant: I told that to the policeman, but he didn't believe me.

## 485

Lawyer to defendant: Do you wish to challenge any of the jury members?
Defendant: Well, I think I could take that guy on the end.

## 486

Why did the dermatologist hurry to the jail?
*Everyone was breaking out.*

## 487

Did you hear about the two hundred stolen mattresses?
*Police are springing into action to find the criminals.*

## 488

In a small town, the chief of police, who was also the veterinarian, was awakened from sleep by a frantic telephone call.

"Please come quick!" said the woman.

"Do you need the police or a vet?" he asked.

"Both," answered the woman. "We can't pry our dog's mouth open, and there's a burglar's leg in it."

## 489

A lawyer and his doctor friend were working out at the gym.

"I come here to exercise, but people are always asking me for advice," the doctor complained to the lawyer. "What do you think I should do?"

"Well," said the lawyer, "the next time you give advice, send a bill."

A few days later, the doctor opened his mail and found a bill—from the lawyer.

## 490

Judge: You have been accused of hitting a comedian with your car, then dragging him four blocks.

Driver: It was only three blocks, Your Honor.

Judge: That's still carrying a joke too far.

## 491

A woman was trying to pull out of her parking space. She first bumped the car behind her, then scraped the car in front, and finally crashed into a truck. A policeman arrived and asked to see her license.

"Don't be silly," she said. "Who would ever give me a license?"

## 492

A police officer was escorting a prisoner to jail when the officer's hat blew off down the sidewalk.

"Would you like me to get that for you?" asked the prisoner.

"You must think I'm an idiot!" said the officer. "You just wait here, and I'll get it."

## 493

A man walked into a bank to hold it up and gave the teller a note that read, "This is a stickup. Give me all your money."

She passed a note back to him that said, "Fix your tie. We're taking your picture."

## 494

Why would Snow White make a great judge?
*Because she is the fairest of them all.*

## 495

A criminal said to the judge, "Your Honor, I'm not guilty. I know I can prove it if you'll just give me some time."

"Sure," replied the judge. "Ten years. Next!"

## 496

The woman pulled her car over to the side of the road when she heard the police car's siren.

"How long have you been driving without a taillight?" demanded the officer.

"Oh, no!" screamed the woman. She jumped out and ran to the back of the car.

"Just calm down," said the officer. "It isn't *that* serious."

"But wait 'til my husband finds out!"

"Where is he?"

"He's in the trailer that was hitched to the car!"

## 497

Judge: Why couldn't you settle this matter your-selves?

Defendant: We tried to, Your Honor, but the police broke it up.

## 498

A man dialed 9-1-1, terrified after his assault.

"I was entering my back door," he reported, "when I was struck on the head. Thankfully, I made it into the house and locked the door. Please send help!"

The dispatcher told him to stay calm, then sent an officer to investigate. The officer soon returned to the station with a large knot on his head.

"That was fast," said the chief. "How did you do it?"

"It was really pretty easy," replied the officer. "I stepped on the rake, too."

## 499

A pizza-shop owner was audited by the IRS.

The agent said, "You have some travel expenses that need to be explained. How do you justify four trips to Rome this year?"

"Oh, I don't need to justify that," replied the shop owner. "Don't you know? We deliver."

## 500

An inmate wrote his wife a letter. "Don't plant the potatoes—that's where I buried the money."

He soon received a reply from his wife. "They censored your letter and have dug up the entire backyard."

He wrote back, "*Now* you can plant the potatoes."

## 501

Alex: Weren't you afraid when the robber pulled a knife on you?

Will: No. I knew he wasn't a professional. The knife still had peanut butter on it.

## 502

Three older ladies were driving down the highway at a very slow speed. A policeman pulled them over and explained that driving so slowly on the highway could be hazardous. The driver explained that she was following the posted limit: 20 miles per hour.

The policeman hid a smile, looking at the sign the woman had indicated. "Ma'am," he said, "that sign indicates that you are traveling on Highway 20."

"Well, that explains why Sally has been so quiet back there," the woman admitted. "From what you've explained, we just turned off Highway 110."

## 503

A man wrote a letter to the IRS: "I have been unable to sleep knowing that I have cheated on my income tax. I understated my taxable income and have enclosed a check for two hundred dollars. If I still can't sleep, I will send the rest."

## 504

Why did the cucumber need a lawyer?
*It was in a pickle.*

## 505

A police officer was investigating an accident on a narrow two-lane road on which the drivers had hit virtually head-on.

One driver, an extremely elderly woman, kept repeating, "He wouldn't let me have my half of the road!"

After gathering as much information as possible, the officer approached the other driver, who was examining his own damage. The police officer said, "That old lady says you wouldn't let her have her half of the road. Why not?"

In exasperation, the man turned from his smashed car and said, "Officer, I would have been more than happy to give her half of the road, if she would have just let me know which half she wanted."

## 506

Heckling in the courtroom had constantly interrupted the trial, and the judge had had enough.

"The next person who interrupts the proceeding will be thrown out of my court!" he said severely, at which the defendant yelled, "Hooray!"

## 507

A group of kindergarteners was on a class outing to their local police station where they saw pictures, tacked to a bulletin board, of the ten most-wanted men.

One of the youngsters pointed to a picture and asked if it really was the photo of a wanted person.

"Yes," answered the policeman.

"Well," wondered the child, "why didn't you keep him when you took his picture?"

## 508

Did you hear about the crimes over at that house they're renovating?

*The shower was stalled while the curtains were held up. Apparently the doors were also hung, and I heard the window was framed for it.*

## 509

A police officer saw a lady driving and knitting at the same time, so after driving next to her for a while, he yelled, "Pull over!"

"No!" she called back. "It's a pair of socks!"

## 510

Why did the strawberry need a lawyer?
*It was in a jam.*

## 511

Did you hear about the calendar thief?
*He got twelve months; they say his days are numbered!*

## 512

A man was speeding down the highway. An officer pulled him over and gave him a ticket. After staring at it, the driver asked, "When's the raffle?"

## 513

"They were causing an awful lot of commotion at the zoo, Your Honor," the zoo attendant said.

"Boys," said the judge sternly, "I never like to hear reports of juvenile delinquency. Now I want each of you to tell me your name and what you were doing wrong."

"My name is George," said the first boy, "and I threw peanuts into the elephant pen."

"My name is Larry," said the second boy, "and I threw peanuts into the elephant pen."

"My name is Mike," said the third boy, "and I threw peanuts into the elephant pen."

"My name is Peanuts," said the fourth boy.

## 514

A man traveling at 120 miles per hour on the interstate was stopped by highway police.

"Sorry, Officer," said the driver. "Was I driving too fast?"

"No, sir. You were flying too low."

## 515

A speeding driver was pulled over by a policeman. The driver asked, "Why was I pulled over when I wasn't the only one speeding?"

The policeman replied, "Have you ever been fishing?"

"Yes," answered the motorist.

"And have you ever caught *all* the fish?"

## 516

"I am not at all satisfied with the evidence against you," said the magistrate to the prisoner on trial, "so I shall find you not guilty. You are free to go."

"Oh, good," said the prisoner. "Does that mean that I can keep the money?"

## 517

What did the police do with the hamburger?
*They grilled it.*

## 518

A young woman is speeding down a freeway, when she is stopped by a highway patrol officer. The officer asks if he can see her driver's license.

The woman replies angrily, "I wish you guys would make up your mind. Just yesterday you take away my license, and now you expect me to show it to you!"

## 519

Matt: What happened to the robber who stole the lamp?
Dave: Oh, he got a very light sentence.

## 520

What did the police officer say when he caught the woman who had stolen the office equipment?
*"Just give me the fax, ma'am."*

## 521

How did the police know the photographer was guilty?
*They found his prints all over the scene of the crime.*

## 522

The traffic cop pulls over a driver who has been speeding and asks him, "Didn't you see the speed limit signs posted along the road?"

"Why, Officer," said the driver, "I was going much too fast to read those tiny little signs."

## 523

Judge: I find you guilty, and I'm giving you a choice: fifteen thousand dollars or six months in jail.
Defendant: Your Honor, I'll take the money!

## 524

The fire department was called to the scene of a large fire. One truck arrived well ahead of the others, with the driver speeding through the streets. He quickly doused the flames.

At a dinner given in the fireman's honor, the mayor gave a speech about how he had saved the building, as well as those around it, by getting there so fast and extinguishing the fire.

"What can we give you to show our gratitude for your work?" asked the mayor.

"Brakes," replied the fireman.

## 525

A woman filling out an accident report wrote: "I had to back out of the driveway, and by the time I had backed out far enough to see if anything was coming, it already had."

## 526

"What is your age?" asked the defense attorney. "Remember, ma'am, you are under oath."

"Twenty-nine years and some months," she answered.

"How many months did you say?" the lawyer interrogated.

In a barely audible voice, she replied, "Three hundred and ten."

## 527

"I have good news and bad news," the defense attorney told his client. "I'll tell you the bad news first. The blood test came back, and your DNA is an exact match with that found at the crime scene."

"Oh, no!" cried the client. "What's the good news?"

"Your cholesterol is only 178."

## 528

What happens to gold when it is exposed to the air?
*It gets stolen.*

## 529

Four elderly ladies came into the pro shop after playing eighteen holes of golf. They appeared to be a bit exhausted. The pro asked, "Did you ladies have a good game today?"

The first lady said, "Well, I had four riders today."

The second lady said, "I had the most riders I've ever had...five."

The third lady said, "I did about the same as last time. I had seven."

The last lady said, "I beat my old record. I had ten riders today. Isn't that great?"

After they had gone into the ladies' locker room, another golfer who had overheard their conversation went to the pro and said, "I have been playing golf for thirty years and thought I knew all the terminology of the game, but what in the world is a *rider*?"

The pro said, "A *rider* occurs when you hit the ball far enough to get in the golf cart and ride to it."

## 530

A man called a lawyer and asked, "How much would you charge for answering three simple questions?"

"Nine hundred dollars," the lawyer replied.

"Nine hundred dollars!" the man exclaimed. "That's a lot, isn't it?"

"Yes, it is," said the lawyer. "Now, what's your third question?"

## 531

Frank and Terrence, two judges, were each arrested on speeding charges. When they arrived in court on the appointed day, no one was there. So instead of wasting time waiting, they decided to try each other. Motioning Frank to the witness stand, Terrence said, "How do you plead?"

"Guilty, Your Honor."

"That'll be fifty dollars and a warning from the court." Terrence stepped down and the judges shook hands and changed places.

"How do you plead?" asked Frank.

"Guilty."

Frank thought for a moment. "These reckless driving cases are becoming all too common," he said. "In fact, this is the second such incident in the last fifteen minutes. That will be three hundred dollars and five days in jail."

## 532

A woman was found guilty in traffic court. When asked for her occupation, she said she was a schoolteacher.

The judge spoke from the bench. "Madam, I have waited years for a schoolteacher to appear before this court." He smiled with delight. "Now sit down at that table and write 'I will not run a red light' five hundred times."

## 533

"The prosecutor says she can produce five witnesses who saw you running from the bank with the money bags," the defense lawyer told his client.

"Oh, that's nothing," said the suspect. "I can produce two hundred witnesses who didn't see me running from the bank."

## 534

Did you hear about the cowboy who wore paper pants, a paper shirt, paper boots, and wore a paper hat? The sheriff arrested him for rustling.

## 535

A rookie police officer was assigned to ride in a cruiser with an experienced partner. A call came over the radio telling them to break up a group of people loitering.

The officers drove to the street and observed a small crowd standing on a corner. The rookie rolled down his window and said, "People, move off this corner!"

No one moved, so he yelled, "Get off this corner *now!*"

Intimidated, the group of people began to leave, looking puzzled. Proud of his first official act, the young policeman turned to his partner and asked, "Okay, how did I do?"

"Not too bad," replied the veteran, "especially since this is a bus stop."

# LOVE AND MARRIAGE

## 536

So I went up to him and said, "Only a coward would hit a woman. Why don't you hit a man?" And that's all I remember.

## 537

John and Nathan were pondering John's problems. "Andrea and I want to get married," said John, "but we can't find anywhere to live."

"Why don't you live with Andrea's parents?" suggested Nathan.

"We can't do that," said John, "they're living with *their* parents!"

## 538

Attending a wedding for the first time, a little girl whispered to her mother, "Why is the bride dressed in white?"

"Because white is the color of happiness," her mother explained, "and today is the happiest day in her life."

The child thought for a moment and then asked, "So why is the groom wearing black?"

## 539

Little Amy confided to her uncle, "When I grow up, I'm going to marry the boy next door."

"Why is that?"

" 'Cause I'm not allowed to cross the road."

## 540

Two antennae decided one day to get married. The wedding wasn't that good, but the reception was great!

## 541

"You just go ahead," said the man to his wife when they got to the mall. "While you're shopping, I'll just look around in the hardware store."

An hour later, she returned and saw him at the checkout counter. The clerk was ringing up the last of a pile of tools and supplies that would fill the car.

"Are you buying all this?" his wife asked him in surprise.

"Well, yes," he said. "But look at all the stuff I'm leaving behind."

## 542

One morning a woman said to her husband, "I bet you don't know what day this is."

"Of course I do," he indignantly answered, going out the door on his way to the office.

At 11:00, the doorbell rang, and when the woman answered it, she was handed a box containing a dozen long-stemmed red roses.

At 1:00, a foil-wrapped box of her favorite chocolates arrived.

Later in the afternoon, a boutique delivered a designer dress.

The woman couldn't wait for her husband to come home. "First the flowers, then the candy, and then the dress!" she exclaimed when he walked in the door. "I've never had a more wonderful Groundhog Day in my whole life!"

## 543

A man was watching a football game, when his wife returned from the mall, loaded down with bags.

"I thought you were only going window-shopping," he said.

"Yes, I bought the curtains for the kitchen window, but I got a few things that match them: a can opener, coffee maker, blender. . ."

## 544

Why did the melon and the honeydew have a big wedding?
*Because they cantaloupe.*

## 545

A man asked his wife, "What would you most like for your birthday?"

She said, "Oh, I'd love to be ten again."

He came up with a plan, and, on the morning of her birthday, he took her to a theme park. They rode every ride in the park together.

Lunchtime soon came, so into McDonald's they went, where she was given a Big Mac with french fries and a milkshake. After lunch, he took her to a movie theater to watch the latest movie for kids—complete with popcorn and soda.

At last she staggered home with her husband and collapsed into bed. Her husband leaned over and asked, "So, sweetheart, what was it like being ten again?"

She looked at him and said quietly, "Actually, I meant the dress size."

## 546

A husband, proving to his wife that women talk more than men, showed her a study that indicated that men use on the average only fifteen thousand words a day, whereas women use thirty thousand words a day.

"Well," she replied, "that's because women have to repeat everything they say when they're talking to men."

"What?" he said.

# MEDICINE

## 547

What do you call the last teeth we get?
*False teeth.*

## 548

Fran: The doctor told me to drink carrot juice after a hot bath.
June: Do you like the carrot juice?
Fran: I don't know yet. I'm still drinking the hot bath.

## 549

Patient: Help me, Doc. I can't remember anything for more than a few minutes. It's driving me crazy!
Doctor: How long has this been going on?
Patient: How long has what been going on?

## 550

I paid more than two thousand dollars to get a cure for my baldness, but I figured it's better to give than to recede.

## 551

A family who lived deep in the woods had no electricity in their home. The wife was about to have her first child, so the father hurried to find a doctor.

At nightfall, the doctor asked the man to bring the lantern.

After their baby girl was delivered, the man put the lantern back on the table.

Suddenly the doctor said, "Hurry, bring the lantern back," and the man complied.

Another baby girl was delivered, and the man returned the lantern to the table.

"Quick," said the doctor. "Bring the light back."

"Doc," said the man, "you don't think they're attracted to the light, do you?"

## 552

A man hurried into the emergency room and asked an intern for a cure for the hiccups. The intern grabbed a cup of water and splashed it onto the man's face.

"What in the world did you do that for?" asked the man.

"Well, you don't have the hiccups anymore, do you?" asked the intern.

"No," he replied. "My wife is in the car—she has them."

## 553

Lois: You said you live off the *spat* of the land. Don't you mean the *fat* of the land?

Glenn: No. I'm a marriage counselor.

## 554

Doctor: After the operation, you'll be a new man.

Patient: Could you send the bill to the old man?

## 555

A man arrived at the emergency room with both of his ears badly burned.

"How did this happen?" the doctor asked.

"I was ironing my shirt when the phone rang, and I answered the iron by mistake," explained the man.

"Well, what about the other ear?" the doctor inquired.

"Oh—that happened when I called for the ambulance."

## 556

Patient: Doctor, I'm really nervous. This is my first operation.
Doctor: I know exactly how you feel. You're my first patient.

## 557

Patient: Why do you whistle when you operate, Doctor?
Doctor: It helps to take my mind off my work.

## 558

Doctor: How is the boy who swallowed the quarter?
Nurse: No change yet.

## 559

Mitch: Why do you have three pairs of glasses?
Dale: One is for driving, the second is for reading, and the third is for looking for the other two.

## 560

Why do surgeons wear masks during an operation?
*So that if any mistake is made, no one will know who did it.*

## 561

Tim: My doctor told me to take something good for my cold.
Todd: So what did you take?
Tim: I took his coat.

## 562

One psychologist greeting another on the street: You're fine, how am I?

## 563

Ralph noticed his life changed dramatically after he got a new hearing aid. Showing it off to his wife, he commented, "This is the world's best hearing aid. As a matter of fact, I can't remember hearing this well since I was a kid."

"Well, what kind is it?" asked his wife.

Ralph glanced at his watch and replied, "Oh, it's about two fifteen."

## 564

A man went to his doctor. When the doctor entered the examining room, the man cried, "My hair is falling out! Can you give me something to keep it in?"

"Of course," said the doctor reassuringly, and he handed the man a small box. "Will this be big enough?"

## 565

A man went to the doctor and said, "Doc, every time I drink coffee, I get terrible pains in my eye."

The doctor said, "Next time, take the spoon out first."

## 566

An old man was afraid that his wife was losing her hearing. So he walked up close to her and asked, "Can you hear me?"

She didn't answer.

He walked up closer and asked again. But there was no answer.

Finally he asked her one more time, really loudly, and his wife said, "For the third time, yes!"

## 567

A young woman went to her doctor, complaining of pain. "Where are you hurting?" asked the doctor.

"I hurt all over," said the woman.

"What do you mean, all over?" asked the doctor. "Be a little more specific."

The woman touched her right knee with her index finger and yelled, "Ow, that hurts." Then she touched her left cheek and again yelled, "Ouch! That hurts, too." Then she touched her right earlobe. "Ow, even *that* hurts," she cried.

The doctor checked her thoughtfully for a moment and told her his diagnosis. "Ma'am, you have a broken finger."

## 568

A man went to see his doctor. The doctor asked what was wrong.

"Doctor," the man said, "I think I'm a moth."

To this the doctor responded, "You think you're a moth? Well, I don't think you need a doctor. Sounds like what you need is a therapist."

"Yeah," said the patient. "I was on my way to see a therapist, but I came in here because I saw your light was on."

## 569

Patient: Doctor, Doctor! My family thinks I'm mad!
Doctor: Why is that?
Patient: I like sausages.
Doctor: There's nothing strange about that. I like sausages, too.
Patient: Really? You must come and see my collection—I've got thousands!

## 570

Patient: Doctor, Doctor! I think I swallowed a spoon!
Doctor: Just sit patiently and try not to stir.

## 571

In the doctor's office, two patients are talking. "You know," says the first, "I had an appendectomy last month, and the doctor left a sponge in me by mistake."

"A sponge!" exclaims the other. "Do you feel much pain?"

"No pain at all," says the first, "but I do get thirstier than I used to!"

## 572

An elderly gentleman had serious hearing problems for a number of years. He went to the doctor and was fitted for a set of hearing aids that allowed the man to hear perfectly.

The elderly gentleman went back in a month to the doctor, and the doctor said, "Your hearing is perfect. Your family must be really pleased you can hear again."

The gentleman replied, "Oh, I haven't told my family yet. I just sit around and listen to their conversations. I've changed my will five times!"

## 573

A woman, on meeting a psychologist at a party, tried to get some free professional advice. "What kind of toy would you suggest giving a little boy on his third birthday?" she asked.

"I'd have to know more about the child," the psychologist answered.

The woman took a deep breath. "He's very bright and quick-witted and exceptionally advanced for his age," she said. "He has good coordination and expresses himself very well."

"Oh, I see," the psychologist said. "It's *your* child!"

## 574

Mr. Johnson was overweight, so his doctor put him on a diet. He said, "I want you to eat regularly for two days, then skip a day, and repeat this procedure for two weeks. The next time I see you, you should have lost at least five pounds."

When Mr. Johnson returned, he shocked the doctor by having dropped almost twenty-five pounds.

"That's incredible!" the doctor told him. "You did this just by following my instructions?"

The slimmed-down Mr. Johnson nodded. "I'll tell you, though, I thought I was going to drop dead that third day."

"From hunger, you mean?"

"No," replied Mr. Johnson, "from skipping."

## 575

The students in a second-grade class were asking their teacher about her newly pierced ears.

"Does the hole go all the way through?"

"Yes."

"Did it hurt?"

"Just a little."

"Did they use a needle?"

"No, they used a special gun."

Silence followed, and then one solemn voice quietly asked, "How far away did they stand?"

## 576

What is the best time to make a dentist appointment?
*Tooth-hurty.*

## 577

Did you hear what happened to the optometrist?
*He fell into his lens grinder and made a spectacle of himself.*

## 578

A man who had just undergone a very complicated operation called the doctor's office to complain about a bump on his head and a terrible headache. Since it had been abdominal surgery, the nurse he spoke with couldn't imagine why he would be complaining of a headache.

The nurse told the patient she would speak with the doctor. She thought perhaps he could be suffering from some postoperative shock.

"Oh, don't worry about it," the doctor told her. "He really does have a bump on his head. About halfway through the operation, we ran out of anesthetic."

## 579

Sydney: I must have sneezed fifty times today. Do you think there's something in the air?
Allen: Yes, your germs!

## 580

A man and wife rushed into a dentist's office. The wife said, "I want a tooth pulled. I don't want any gas or numbing cream because I'm in a terrible hurry. Just pull the tooth as quickly as possible."

"You certainly are a brave woman," said the dentist. "Now, show me which tooth it is."

The wife turned to her husband and said, "Open your mouth and show the dentist which tooth it is, dear."

## 581

A new nurse listened while the doctor was yelling, "Typhoid! Tetanus! Measles!"

"Why is he doing that?" she asked another nurse.

"Oh, he just likes to call the shots around here," she replied.

## 582

A man returns from an overseas trip feeling very ill. He goes to see his doctor and is immediately rushed to the hospital to undergo a barrage of tests.

The man wakes up after the tests in a private room at the hospital. The phone by his bed rings.

"Hello. This is your doctor. We have received the results from your tests. We've found you have an extremely contagious virus."

"Oh, no!" cried the man. "What are you going to do?"

"Well," said the doctor, "we're going to put you on a diet of pizzas, pancakes, and pita bread."

"And that will cure me?" asked the man.

The doctor replied, "Well, no, but it's the only food we can slide under the door."

## 583

An accountant is having a hard time sleeping and goes to see his doctor.

"Doctor, I just can't get to sleep at night."

"Have you tried counting sheep?"

"That's the problem. I make a mistake and then spend three hours trying to find it."

# MUSICAL NOTES

## 584

In what key is "Exploring the Cave with No Flashlight" written?
*C sharp or B flat.*

## 585

A note left for a pianist from his wife: *Gone Chopin, have Liszt, Bach in a minuet.*

## 586

How do you make a bandstand?
*Pull their chairs away.*

## 587

How is a heart like a musician?
*They both have a beat.*

## 588

Why couldn't the bell keep a secret?
*It always tolled.*

## 589

Ian: My neighbors were screaming and yelling at three o'clock this morning!
Mark: Did they wake you?
Ian: Nah. . .I was already up, playing my bagpipes.

## 590

Why do refrigerators hum?
*Because they don't know the words.*

## 591

What do Tarzan and Jane sing at Christmastime?
*"Jungle Bells."*

## 592

The high school band was nervous. So was the new music teacher. As they were preparing for their first concert, he told the kids that if they weren't sure of their part, just to pretend to play.

When the big night arrived, the proud parents waited expectantly. The teacher brought down the baton with a flourish, and lo, the band gave forth with a resounding silence.

# POTPOURRI

## 593

What is taken before you get it?
*Your picture.*

## 594

What can you hold without touching it?
*Your breath.*

## 595

What never moves, has no feet, but wears shoes?
*A sidewalk.*

## 596

How does Bill Gates enter his house?
*He uses Windows.*

## 597

What has neither flesh nor bone, but has four fingers and a thumb?
*A glove.*

## 598

What goes up but never comes down?
*Your age.*

## 599

Why are Saturday and Sunday so strong?
*Because the rest are weekdays.*

## 600

What did the tie say to the hat?
*"You go on ahead while I hang around."*

## 601

What question can never be answered by "Yes"?
*"Are you asleep?"*

## 602

What is the only thing you break when you say its name?
*Silence.*

## 603

What did the bald man say when he received a comb for his birthday?
*"Thank you very much. I'll never part with it."*

## 604

What is the difference between ignorance, apathy, and ambivalence?
*I don't know, and I don't care one way or the other.*

## 605

Why is it that you always find what you're looking for in the last place you look?
*You stop looking for it after you find it.*

## 606

What can you not see, even though it is always before you?
*The future.*

## 607

What did Snow White say when her photos didn't come back from the photo store?
*"Some day my prints will come!"*

## 608

What do you put in a barrel to make it lighter?
*A hole.*

## 609

A man is locked in a room with no way to get out. In the room there is a piano, a baseball bat, a saw, and a table. How could he get out?
*He could take a key from the piano and unlock the door. He could take the bat and get three strikes. Then he'd be out. He could take the saw and cut the table in two. Then, by putting the two halves together, he would have a "hole" and he could get out.*

## 610

What gets wetter and wetter as it dries?
*A towel.*

# 611

Where is the shortest bridge in the world?
*On your nose.*

# 612

What's faster—hot or cold?
*Hot is, because you can catch a cold.*

# 613

A speaker was scheduled to address an audience at a university. A couple of hours before she was to take the podium, some student pranksters took all of the folding chairs, loaded them into their vehicles, and drove away. No one was aware of the problem until the audience began arriving for the lecture. There wasn't enough time to find more chairs, so everyone had to stand while she spoke.

That evening, she decided to write to her mother to let her know how the speech went. "It was a huge success," she wrote. "Hours before I arrived, every seat in the house was taken, and I was given a standing ovation throughout my speech."

# 614

Earl: Can you keep a secret?
Pam: Sure, but I can't promise the people I tell it to can!

# 615

What do you call a man down in a hole?
*Doug.*

# 616

What do you call a man who hangs on a wall?
*Art.*

# 617

What goes up and down but doesn't move?
*A staircase.*

# 618

What goes around the yard but never moves?
*A fence.*

## 619

What did one magnet say to the other?
*"I find you very attractive."*

## 620

What can you hold without ever touching it?
*A conversation.*

## 621

What is the invention that allows you to see through
the thickest walls?
*The window.*

## 622

How can you safely jump off a thirty-foot ladder?
*Jump from the bottom rung.*

## 623

What did the plug say to the wall?
*"Socket to me!"*

## 624

Brett: Do you have holes in your socks?
Jim: Certainly not!
Brett: Then how do you get your feet in them?

## 625

What did one eye say to the other eye?
*"Something's come between us that smells."*

# SENIOR MOMENTS

## 626

A man moved to a nursing home. He soon noticed that a woman was constantly staring at him. After a few days, he approached her and asked, "Ma'am, why have you been staring at me all the time?"

"You look just like my third husband," she replied.

"Well, how many times have you been married?" he asked.

She answered, "Twice."

## 627

Three elderly sisters are sitting in the living room, chatting about various things. One sister says, "You know, I'm getting really forgetful. This morning, I was standing at the top of the stairs, and I couldn't remember whether I had just come up or was about to go down."

The second sister says, "You think that's bad? The other day, I was sitting on the edge of my bed, and I couldn't remember whether I was going to bed or had just woken up!"

The third sister smiles smugly. "Well, my memory's just as good as it's always been, knock on wood." She raps on the table. "You sit still. I'll answer the door."

## 628

Two old-timers were chatting at a restaurant. One said, "Hey, Max, isn't this your fiftieth anniversary?"

Max replied, "Yep."

"Well," his friend inquired, "what are you planning on doing?"

Max replied, "Well, I remember taking my wife to Arizona on our twenty-fifth anniversary."

"Hmm," the friend said, "you'll have to do something special for your fiftieth. What are you going to do?"

"I guess," Max answered, "I'll go back to pick her up."

## 629

A lady fell into the water, and not being a swimmer, she called for help. A man jumped in to save her and grabbed her by the hair, but she was wearing a wig, and it came off.

He then grabbed her by the chin, and her false teeth popped out.

The man then yelled, "Somebody help me save all of this woman that we can!"

## 630

Two elderly couples were enjoying a friendly conversation, when one of the men asked the other, "Fred, how was the memory clinic you went to last month?"

"Fantastic," Fred replied. "They taught us all the latest psychological techniques: visualization, association. . .it was great."

"That's terrific! And what was the name of the clinic?"

Fred went blank. He thought and thought, but he couldn't remember. Then a smile broke across his face and he asked, "What do you call that flower with the long stem and thorns?"

"You mean a rose?"

"Yes, that's it!" He turned to his wife. "Rose, what was the name of that memory clinic?"

## 631

At a fancy reception, a young man was asked by a widow to guess her age.

"You must have some idea of how old I am," she urged, as he hesitated.

"I have several ideas," he said with a smile. "I just don't know whether to make it ten years younger because of your looks or ten years older because of your intelligence."

## 632

While on a road trip, an elderly couple stopped at a roadside restaurant for lunch. After finishing their meal, they left the restaurant and resumed their trip.

Unfortunately, the elderly woman had left her glasses on the table, and she didn't miss them until after they had been driving about thirty minutes. Then, to add to the aggravation, they had to travel quite a distance farther before they could find a place to turn around.

All the way back, the elderly husband fussed and scolded his wife.

They finally arrived at the restaurant, and as the woman got out of the car and hurried inside to retrieve her glasses, the man yelled to her, "While you're in there, you might as well get my hat, too."

## 633

A reporter interviewed a 103-year-old woman.

"And what is the best thing about being 103?" the reporter asked.

She simply replied, "No peer pressure."

# 634

Three elderly men are at the doctor's office for a memory test. The doctor asks the first man, "What is three times three?"

"Two hundred and eighteen," comes the reply.

The doctor rolls his eyes, looks up at the ceiling, and says to the second man, "It's your turn. What is three times three?"

"Friday," replies the second man.

The doctor shakes his head sadly, then asks the third man, "Okay, your turn. What is three times three?"

"Nine," says the third man.

"That's great!" says the doctor. "How did you get that answer?"

"Simple," he says, "just subtract 218 from Friday."

# SPACE AND
# NATURE

## 635

Greg: Which is farther, Australia or the moon?
Pete: Australia. You can see the moon at night.

## 636

What is not a plant, but sometimes has leaves?
*A table.*

## 637

Did you hear about the restaurant on the moon?
*Great food, but no atmosphere.*

## 638

If the lightning scares you, don't worry; it will be over in a flash.

## 639

The more you take away, the bigger it gets—what is it?
*A hole.*

## 640

A man writing to the meteorologist: I thought you may be interested in knowing that I shoveled eighteen inches of "partly cloudy" from my sidewalk this morning.

## 641

What can pass in front of the sun without making a shadow?
*The wind.*

## 642

Have you heard about the man who sat up all night trying to figure out where the sun went when it set?
*It finally dawned on him.*

## 643

How does the Man on the Moon get his hair cut?
*Eclipse it.*

## 644

What kind of waves are impossible to swim in?
*Microwaves.*

## 645

What part of the keyboard do astronauts like best?
*The space bar.*

## 646

What is brown and sticky?
*A stick.*

## 647

Why did the atom cross the road?
*Because it was time to split.*

## 648

What did the sun say when it was introduced to the Earth?
*"Pleased to heat you."*

## 649

How do you get an astronaut's baby to fall asleep?
*Rocket.*

## 650

What's the difference between Neptune and Earth?
*There's a world of difference!*

## 651

One astronaut asks another astronaut if he has ever heard of the planet Saturn.

The second astronaut says, "I'm not sure, but it has a familiar ring."

## 652

A tourist was admiring the necklace worn by a local Indian.

"What is that made of?" she asked.

"Alligator's teeth," the Indian replied.

"I'm guessing they mean as much to you as pearls do to us," she said.

"Oh no," he objected. "Anyone can open an oyster."

## 653

What do you get when you mix poison ivy with a four-leaf clover?
*A rash of good luck.*

## 654

What is one thing you can never catch?
*A breeze.*

## 655

How can you carry water in a net?
*Freeze it.*

## 656

What kind of bow is impossible to tie?
*A rainbow.*

## 657

It's a small world, but I wouldn't want to have to vacuum it.

## 658

In November, the Indian chief began to think it was going to be a cold winter. So he instructed his tribe to collect firewood. To double-check his prediction, the chief called the National Weather Service and asked a meteorologist if the winter was going to be a cold one.

The man responded, "According to our indicators, we think it just might be."

Following the phone call, the chief told his people to find extra wood, just in case. A week later he called the National Weather Service again, and they confirmed that a harsh winter was indeed headed their way.

The chief ordered all of the villagers to scavenge every scrap of wood they could. Two weeks later, he called the National Weather Service again and asked, "Are you absolutely certain this winter is going to be very cold?"

"Oh, we sure are," the man replied. "The Indians are collecting wood like crazy."

## 659

What tree is always unhappy?
*The blue spruce.*

## 660

What doesn't get any wetter no matter how hard it rains?
*The ocean.*

## 661

Tell a man there are three hundred billion stars in the universe, and he believes you. Tell him a bench has wet paint on it, and he has to touch it to be sure.

# SPORTS AND LEISURE

## 662

What's the biggest diamond in the world?
*A baseball diamond.*

## 663

What does an umpire do when he gets a headache?
*Takes two aspirins and calls as little as possible.*

## 664

What is the best day of the week to play a double-header?
*Tuesday.*

## 665

Park ranger: What's wrong?
Camper: I have a camouflage tent.
Park ranger: What's wrong with that?
Camper: I've looked everywhere, and I just can't find it.

## 666

Guide: I don't guide hunters anymore, only fishermen.
Hunter: Why?
Guide: I have never been mistaken for a fish.

## 667

What is the best kind of shoes to wear for stealing bases?
*Sneakers.*

## 668

Hunter 1: We're lost. Shoot three shots in the air.
Hunter 2: Okay.
Hunter 1: If no one comes soon, go ahead and shoot three more.
Hunter 2: I hope someone comes soon. We're getting low on arrows.

## 669

One hunter to another: Look at those bear tracks! I'll go see where he came from, and you can go see where he went.

## 670

Did you hear about the hunter who had a close call? He saw some tracks and went over to look at them closely. That's when the train almost hit him.

# 671

Exhausted hiker: I am so glad to see you! I've been lost for three days!

Other hiker: Well, don't get too excited. I've been lost for a week.

# 672

The room was full of pregnant women and their partners. The Lamaze class was in full swing. The instructor was teaching the women how to breathe properly, and informing the men how to give the support and encouragement needed.

"Ladies, exercise is good for you," announced the teacher. "Walking is especially beneficial. And, gentlemen, it would be great for you to take the time to go walking with your partner!"

A man in the middle of the group spoke up. "Is it all right if she carries a golf bag while we walk?"

# 673

Mom: Where's your brother?

Sam: Well, if the ice is as thick as he thinks it is, he's skating. But if it's as thin as I think it is, he's swimming.

# 674

A mother scolded her son for not being fair with his little brother. "You need to let him have a turn with your skateboard," she said.

"Mom, I have," he told her. "I ride it down the hill, and he gets to ride it up the hill."

# 675

On her way back from the concession stand, Marge asked a man at the end of the row, "Excuse me, but did I step on your foot a few minutes ago?"

Expecting an apology, the man said, "Yes, you did."

Marge nodded. "Oh, good. Then this is my row."

# 676

Two fishermen were tossed overboard in rough, stormy weather and found themselves surrounded by sharks. As the sharks argued over which one got the first pick, a lawyer shark swam over and offered some counsel.

"I'll help settle this," said the lawyer shark to the fishermen. "But it will cost you an arm and a leg."

## 677

A parachute jumper prepared for his first jump.

"Don't forget," reminded the instructor, "if the first cord doesn't work, pull the backup cord. Ready?"

"I'm ready!" said the jumper. He jumped, counted to ten, then pulled the cord. Nothing happened, so he pulled the backup cord. But still, nothing happened.

As he fell toward earth, a woman suddenly flew past him, up into the sky.

"Hey!" he yelled. "Do you know anything about parachutes?"

"No," she called back. "Do you know anything about gas stoves?"

## 678

Harry: What would you get if you crossed a baseball
     player with a Boy Scout?
Tom: I don't know, but I bet he sure could pitch a
     tent.

## 679

Parachute recall notice: On page 7 of instruction manual, please change the words "state zip code" to "pull rip cord."

# 680

George came home from a game of golf, and his neighbor asked how he did.

"Oh, I shot seventy," said George.

"That's great!" commended the neighbor.

"Yeah," George said, "and tomorrow I'll play the second hole."

# 681

What's the best hockey team in the universe?
*The All-Stars.*

# 682

Larry was eighty years old and could hit a great round of golf, but his eyesight was failing, and he couldn't see where the ball landed. He asked Bill to go with him. Bill could no longer hit the ball, but his eyes were perfect. Larry hit the ball and turned to Bill and asked, "Did you see where the ball landed?"

Bill replied, "Oh, yes."

"Well," said Larry, "where is it?"

"I forget," said Bill.

## 683

Two old buddies went fishing, and one lost his dentures over the side of the boat. His prankster friend removed his own false teeth, tied them on his line, and pretended he had caught them.

Unhooking the teeth, his grateful mate tried to put them into his mouth, then hurled them into the lake with the disgust. "They're not mine! They don't fit!"

## 684

Why did the football coach go to the bank?
*To get the quarter back.*

## 685

One day, a grandpa and his grandson went golfing. The grandson played a good game of golf, but his grandpa still gave him tips along the way.

When they got to the eighth hole, the grandpa said, "When I was your age, I would hit the ball right over that tree."

So the grandson hit the ball, and it bumped against the tree and landed not too far from where it had started.

"Of course," said the grandpa, "when I was your age, the tree was only three feet tall."

## 686

What can you catch but not throw?
*A cold.*

## 687

Brian and Randy were talking about their golf games. Brian said, "I got kicked off the course today for breaking sixty."

Randy looked at him, amazed. "Breaking sixty? That's incredible!"

Brian smiled and said, "Yeah, I never knew a golf cart could go that fast!"

## 688

Bob and Tom both like to golf. One day Bob went to Tom and said, "Hey, look at this great ball!"

Tom replied, "What's so great about it?"

"Well," Bob said, "if you lose it, it will beep until you find it, and if it goes into the water, it will float. This ball is impossible to lose!"

"Wow!" said Tom. "Where did you get that from?"

Bob replied, "I found it."

## 689

Mother had just finished waxing the floors when she heard her young son opening the front door. She shouted, "Be careful on that floor, Jimmy; it's just been waxed."

Jimmy, walking right in, replied, "Don't worry, Mom, I'm wearing my cleats."

## 690

One day a math teacher and his brother were out golfing. The brother was to tee off first, and just before he swung, he yelled, "Fore!"

The math teacher was up next, and just before he swung, he yelled, "Square root of sixty-four divided by two!"

## 691

More than anything, a young man from the city wanted to be a cowboy. Eventually he found a rancher who took pity on him and gave him a chance.

"This," he said, showing him a rope, "is called a lariat. We use it to catch the cows."

"Hmm," said the man, "and what do you use for bait?"

## 692

Two brothers, Shawn and Curt, went fishing. Every time Shawn threw his hook in, he caught a fish, but Curt didn't have the same success.

By the end of the day, Shawn had caught twelve fish, but Curt had caught nothing.

The next day, Curt woke up very early in the morning, dressed in Shawn's clothes, and carried Shawn's rod. He went to the river and sat where Shawn normally sat. He threw the hook in and waited.

Darkness cleared and the sun rose. After about two hours of waiting, a fish popped out and asked him, "Where is Shawn?"

## 693

Dad: What happened to your eye?
Keith: I was staring at a ball from afar, and I was wondering why it was getting bigger and bigger. Then, it hit me.

## 694

I had lunch with a chess champion the other day. It took him twenty minutes to pass the salt.

## 695

One cold winter day, two guys were ice fishing about twenty feet apart.

The first guy wasn't having any luck. The second guy was pulling out a fish every time he put his line in the water. This made the first guy curious. "Hey," he yelled to the other, "what are you using for bait?"

The other guy yelled back, "Mphh mphh oggth mfft phrr brrt wmmm."

The first guy was very puzzled and said, "What?"

Again the second guy yelled back, "Mphh mphh oggth mfft phrr brrt wmmm."

Finally the first guy had to know what the other guy was saying, so he got up and walked over to him and said, "I couldn't understand a word. What were you saying?"

The second guy spit something into his hand and replied, "I said, you have to keep your bait warm."

## 696

"Hey, you!" yelled the ranger to the small child. "Can't you read that sign? No fishing in this river!"

"I'm not fishing!" came the perky reply. "I'm teaching my worm how to swim!"

# 697

Two would-be fishermen rented a boat, and one caught a large fish.

"We should mark the spot," he said.

The second man drew a large $X$ in the bottom of the boat with a black maker.

"That's no good," said the first man. "Next time out, we may not get the same boat."

# 698

Why don't matches play baseball?
*One strike and they're out.*

# 699

What do you throw out when you need it and take in when you don't need it?
*An anchor.*

# 700

A fisherman accidentally left his day's catch under the seat of a bus. The next evening's newspaper carried an ad: If the person who left a bucket of fish on the number 47 bus would care to come to the garage, he can have the bus.

# 701

Why does it take longer to run from second base to third base than it does from first to second?
*Because there's a shortstop between second and third.*

# 702

Why was Cinderella thrown off the baseball team?
*She kept running away from the ball.*

# 703

What is a diver's favorite game?
*Pool.*

# 704

What do you call a boomerang that doesn't work?
*A stick.*

# 705

What is the best city to go bike riding in?
*Wheeling, West Virginia.*

## 706

What is the best mountain to climb to get a good night's sleep?
*Mount Ever-rest.*

## 707

What do you call four bullfighters in quicksand?
*Quatro sinko.*

## 708

One day, Dylan Wolfe went to play at a different golf course where no one knew him, just to get away and see if he could do better elsewhere.

He hired a caddy to guide him around the course. After another day of slices, duff shots, and misread putts, he was obviously upset. He turned to the caddy and said, "You know, I must be the worst golfer in the world."

"No, sir," the caddy comforted him. "I have heard there is a guy named Dylan Wolfe from across town who is the worst player in the world!"

## 709

If athletes get athlete's foot, then what do astronauts get?
*Missile toe.*

# 710

A salesman, tired of his job, gave it up to become a policeman. Several months later, a friend asked him how he liked his new career.

"Well," he replied, "the pay could be better, and the hours can be long, but what I like about it is that the customer is always wrong."

# 711

Somewhat skeptical of his son's newfound determination to work out, the father nevertheless took his teenager to the sports-equipment store to look at the weight sets.

"Please, Dad," begged the boy, "I promise I'll use them every day."

"I don't know, Justin. It's a big commitment," the father told him.

"I know, Dad," the boy replied.

"They're not cheap either," the father continued.

"I'll use them, Dad, I promise. You'll see."

Finally won over, the father paid for the equipment, and they headed for the door.

From the sidewalk, he heard his son whimper, "What! You mean I have to carry them all the way to the car?"

## 712

Two serious fishermen were out in the middle of the lake. For two hours neither of them moved a muscle. Then one became restless.

"Joe," said his buddy, "that's the second time you've moved your foot in twenty-five minutes. Did you come out here to fish or dance?"

## 713

The football team was losing badly. In desperation, the coach ran over to his worst player and said, "I want you to go out there and get mean and tough!"

"Okay, Coach!" said the player. He jumped to his feet and asked, "Which one's Mean and which one's Tough?"

## 714

He had hoped the situation would eventually resolve itself, but finally the good-humored boss was compelled to call Mr. Brown into his office.

"It has not escaped my attention," he pointed out, "that every time there's a home game at the stadium, you have to take your aunt to the doctor."

Mr. Brown looked incredulous, then responded, "You know, you're right, sir. I didn't realize it. You don't suppose she's faking it, do you?"

# 715

Two friends, one an optimist and the other a pessimist, could never quite agree on any topic of discussion.

The optimist owned a hunting dog that could walk on water. He had a plan: Take the pessimist and the dog out duck hunting in a boat.

They got out to the middle of the lake, and the optimist brought down a duck. The dog immediately walked out across the water, retrieved the duck, and walked back to the boat.

The optimist looked at his friend and said, "What do you think about that?"

The pessimist replied, "That dog can't swim, can he?"

# 716

A businessman who frequently left the office to play golf instructed his secretary to tell all callers only that he was away from his desk. After he left the office one day, a member of his foursome forgot which course they were playing at, so he called for the information.

The loyal secretary would only reply that her boss was away from his desk.

"Please tell me," said the exasperated golfer, "is he five miles away at the country club or ten miles away at Graystone?"

## 777

How is a crossword puzzle like an argument?
*One word leads to another.*

## 718

A wealthy woman was giving a garden party with several well-to-do guests attending. During the festivities, two gardeners were out on the back lawn working. One gardener was busy weeding, when the other suddenly leaped high into the air and spun around.

Taken by his grace, a guest remarked to the host, "That man is such a talented dancer! I'll pay him five hundred dollars to dance at my next party!"

When the host asked the first gardener about such an arrangement, he yelled, "Hey, Louis! Do you think for five hundred bucks you could step on that rake again?"

## 719

Troy: I'm a very famous speaker. I spoke at the Boston Gardens to thousands of people.
Paul: Really? What did you say?
Troy: Get your peanuts, popcorn, and cold drinks here!

# 720

A golfer is playing a round with his buddies. On the sixth hole, a hole over water, he proceeds to hit six balls into the water. Frustrated over his poor golfing, he heaves his golf clubs into the water and begins to walk off the course.

Suddenly he turns around, jumps into the lake, and dives under the water. His buddies think he has changed his mind and is going to retrieve his clubs. But when he comes out of the water, he doesn't have his bag or clubs.

As the wet golfer walks away, one of his buddies asks, "Why did you jump into the lake?"

The man responds, "I left my car keys in the bag."

# 721

Why did the golfer wear two pairs of pants?
*In case he got a hole in one.*

# 722

Why is tennis a noisy game?
*Because when you play it, you have to raise a racket.*

## 723

Kim said to her friend, "I just don't understand the attraction golf holds for men."

"I know!" Rachel responded. "I went golfing with Roger one time, and he told me I asked too many questions."

"I'm sure you were just trying to understand the game. What questions did you ask?"

"Oh, just things like, 'Why did you hit the ball into that lake?'"

## 724

A man is walking from the lake carrying two fish in a bucket. He is approached by the game warden, who asks to see his fishing license.

The fisherman says to the warden, "I did not catch these fish; they are my pets. Every day I come down to the water and whistle, and these fish jump out, and I take them around to see the sights, only to return them at the end of the day."

The warden, not believing a word of it, reminds him that it is illegal to fish without a license. The fisherman turns to the warden and says, "If you don't believe me, then just watch." He then throws the fish into the water.

The warden says, "Now whistle to your fish and show me that they will come out of the water."

"What fish?" asks the fisherman.

## 725

Two men are talking at work Monday morning. "What did you do last weekend?"

"Dropped hooks into water."

"Went fishing, huh?"

"No, golfing."

## 726

Many golfers prefer a golf cart to a caddy because the cart cannot count, criticize, or laugh.

## 727

Two men went duck hunting with their dogs but were having no success.

"I think I figured out what we're doing wrong," said the first hunter.

"Oh, yeah? What's that?" asked the other.

"We're not throwing the dogs high enough."

# TRAVEL AND TRANSPORTAION

## 728

An insurance man was teaching his teenage daughter how to drive. Suddenly the brakes failed.

"I can't stop," she wailed. "What should I do?"

"Don't panic," her father told her. "Just hit something cheap."

## 729

Why doesn't a bike stand up by itself?
*Because it's two-tired.*

## 730

Customer: When I bought this car, you guaranteed that you would fix anything that broke.
Car dealer: Yes, that's right.
Customer: Well, I need a new garage.

## 731

A father, teaching his teenage son to drive: Remember, stop on red, go on green, and take it easy when I turn purple.

## 732

What driver does not need a license?
*A screwdriver.*

## 733

Why do people park in a driveway but drive on a parkway?

## 734

Passenger: Are you sure this train stops at San Francisco?
Conductor: If it doesn't, you'll hear an awful splash.

## 735

Before takeoff, a flight attendant made a general announcement to all passengers. "Please let me know if any of you would like some gum before takeoff. It will prevent your ears from popping as we climb."

After the flight, everyone left except one man.

"Do you need some assistance?" she asked.

"Can you speak up?" he yelled. "I can't hear you with this gum in my ears."

# 736

A man was trying to teach his daughter to drive. Suddenly she screamed, "What do I do now? Here comes a telephone pole!"

# 737

A man at the airline counter tells the woman behind the desk, "I'd like this bag to go to London, this one to Seattle, and this one to Quebec."

"I'm sorry, sir. We can't do that," she replied.

"I'm sure you can," he answered. "That's what you did the last time I flew with you."

# 738

A tourist was driving down a desert road and came upon a sign that said, ROAD CLOSED. DO NOT ENTER. He thought the road looked passable, so he ignored the sign and continued driving down the road.

A mile later, he came to a bridge that was out. He turned around and drove back in the direction he came from. As he approached the warning sign, he read on the other side: WELCOME BACK. TOLD YOU SO!

## 739

Son: Mom, Dad left for work without his glasses, didn't he?
Mom: Yes. How did you know?
Son: The garage door is missing.

## 740

Mr. and Mrs. Roberts had reached the airport just in the nick of time to catch the plane for their vacation in the Bahamas. "I wish we'd brought the piano with us," said Mr. Roberts.

"Why on earth would we bring the piano?" asked his wife.

"I left the tickets on it."

## 741

A motorist got his car stuck in the mud while on a drive through the country. A farmer happened to be by the side of the road and offered to pull him out for twenty dollars.

"At that price, I would think you'd be busy day and night, pulling people out," said the motorist.

"Oh, I can't at night," said the farmer. "That's when I haul water for this hole."

# 742

Bart: What do you call a red-headed woman on a blue-and-white plane flying from New York to London?
Art: A passenger.

# 743

In 1940, two men were flying from New York to Los Angeles on what was then a new DC-3. They left New York, and when they landed in Philadelphia, a red truck drove up to put fuel into the wing.

A short time later, they landed in Pittsburgh, and again, a red truck pulled up to fill the tanks with fuel.

Each time they landed to discharge or take on passengers, a red truck would pull up and add fuel to the tanks. Finally, after landing in Kansas City and seeing the truck pull up again, the first man said to the other, "We sure are making good time."

"Yes, we are," said the second one, "and so is that red truck!"

# 744

What is the hardest thing about learning to ride a bike?
*The pavement.*

## 745

Three old pilots are walking on the ramp. First one says, "Windy, isn't it?"

Second one says, "No, it's Thursday!"

Third one says, "So am I. Let's go get a drink."

## 746

A man went to the airline counter. The ticket agent asked, "Sir, do you have reservations?"

He replied, "Reservations? Of course I have reservations, but I'm flying anyway."

## 747

Flight attendant's request following a less-than-perfect landing: We ask you to please remain seated as Captain Kangaroo bounces us to the terminal.

## 748

What do you call a laughing motorcycle?
*Yamaha-ha-ha.*

# 749

"I've never flown before," the nervous old lady told the pilot. "You will bring me down safely, won't you?"

"All I can say, ma'am," said the pilot, "is that I've never left anyone up there yet!"

# 750

What sits on the bottom of the ocean and twitches?
*A nervous wreck.*

# 751

Did you hear about the red ship and the blue ship that collided?
*The sailors were marooned.*

# 752

Flight attendant's arrival announcement: We'd like to thank you folks for flying with us today. And the next time you get the insane urge to go blasting through the skies in a pressurized metal tube, we hope you'll think of us.

## 753

Through the pitch-black night, the captain sees a light dead ahead on a collision course with his ship. He sends a signal: "Change your course ten degrees east."

The light signals back: "Change yours ten degrees west."

Angry, the captain sends another signal: "I'm a navy captain! Change your course, sir!"

"I'm a seaman, second class," comes the reply. "Change your course, sir."

Now the captain is furious. "I'm a battleship! I'm not changing course!"

There is one last reply: "I'm a lighthouse. It's your call."

## 754

A teenager told his father, "There's trouble with the car. It has water in the carburetor."

The father looked confused and said, "Water in the carburetor? That's ridiculous."

But the son insisted. "The car has water in the carburetor."

His father started to get a little agitated. "You don't even know what a carburetor is," he said. "I'll check it out. Where is the car?"

"In the pool."

# 755

The parents of a difficult boy were discussing what to give him for a birthday present. The mother said, "Let's buy him a bicycle."

"Well," said the father, "maybe, but do you think it will improve his behavior?"

"Probably not," said the mother, "but it will spread it over a wider area."

# 756

Martin had just received his brand-new driver's license. The family trooped out to the driveway and climbed into the car, with Martin in the driver's seat, ready to take them for a ride for the first time. His father was in the backseat, directly behind the newly minted driver.

"I'll bet you're back there to get a change of scenery after all those months of sitting in the front seat, teaching me how to drive," said the boy to his father.

"Nope," came his father's reply, "I'm gonna sit here and kick the back of your seat as you drive, just like you've been doing to me all these years."

## 757

It was raining, the windshield had mud splattered on it, and the car had almost collided with another vehicle twice. The hitchhiker was beginning to wish that this driver hadn't picked him up.

"Don't you think you should wipe off the windshield?" asked the passenger.

"Oh, no," said the motorist with a smile. "That wouldn't do a bit of good. I left my glasses at home."

## 758

The villager on his first trip to the city was waiting at a bus stop. After some hesitation, he asked a woman, "Which bus should I take to the capital?"

"Bus number 143," the woman replied, then boarded her bus.

Later that evening, the woman got off a bus at the same stop and found the villager still waiting.

"Didn't you get the bus to the capital?" she asked.

"Nope, not yet," he replied. "So far, 136 buses have come—only seven more buses before mine arrives."

# 759

Two guys are in a car. The driver comes to a stoplight and goes right through it.

His friend says, "What are you doing?"

The driver says, "It's okay; my brother does it all the time."

They come up to another stoplight and go right through. His friend says, "You are out of your mind."

The driver says, "It's okay; my brother does it all the time."

They come up to a green light and he stops. His friend says, "It's green—go."

The driver replies, "Oh, no, I can't. My brother might be coming!"

# 760

Two guys on a tandem bike were pedaling up a hill. It took forever to get to the top. When they finally got to the top the first guy said in a pant, "Whew, that was so hard."

The second replied, "If I hadn't been pushing the brakes the whole time, we would have rolled down backwards."

## 761

A man whose son had just passed his driving test went home one evening and found that the boy had driven into the living room.

"How on earth did you manage to do that?" he fumed.

"Quite simple, Dad. I came in through the kitchen and turned left!"

## 762

From a passenger ship, everyone can see a bearded man on a small island who is shouting and desperately waving his hands.

"Who is it?" a passenger asks the captain.

"I have no idea. Every year when we pass, he goes crazy."

## 763

A riverboat captain, wanting to put his passengers at ease, said, "I've sailed boats on this river for so long, I know where each sandbar is."

Suddenly the boat struck a sandbar so hard, it shook the boat and all the passengers. "Look," he said, "there's one of them now!"

### 764

What comes once in a minute, once in a month, but never in a day?
*The letter* m.

### 765

A magazine photographer was assigned to get photos of a forest fire. Smoke at the scene was too thick to get any good shots, so he called his office to request a plane. "I'll have it waiting for you at the airport," his editor assured.

As soon as he arrived at the airport, sure enough, there was a plane near the runway. He jumped in with his equipment and yelled, "Let's go!"

The pilot took off, and soon they were in the air. "Fly over the north side of the fire," said the photographer, "and make three low-level passes."

"Why?" asked the pilot.

"Because I'm going to take pictures!" the photographer said with great exasperation.

After a long pause, the pilot said, "You mean you're not the instructor?"

### 766

Phil: Did you lose your train of thought?
Carl: No, but I think one of the cars just derailed.

# 767

A lady went to an auto-parts store and asked for a seven-ten cap. All the clerks looked at each other, and one said, "What's a seven-ten cap?"

She said, "You know, it's right on the engine. Mine got lost somehow and I need a new one."

"What kind of a car is it on?" the clerk asked.

"My 2000 Toyota," she replied.

"Well, how big is it?"

She made a circle with her hands about three-and-a-half inches in diameter.

The clerk asked, "What does it do?"

"I don't know, but it's always been there."

At this point, the manager came over. He handed her a notepad and asked her if she could draw a picture of it. The customer carefully drew a circle about three-and-a-half inches in diameter. In the center she writes, "710."

The manager, looking at the drawing upside down, walked to a shelf and grabbed an OIL cap.

# 768

Navy jet pilot: This is it! We're flying faster than the speed of sound!
Copilot: What?

# 769

A man and his wife had an argument one evening and weren't speaking to each other afterward. He had a business flight in the morning, so before he went to bed, he wrote a note reading, "Please wake me at 5:00 a.m.," and left it on her pillow.

The next morning the man woke up to discover it was 7:00 and that he had missed his flight. Furious, he was about to go confront his wife, when he noticed a piece of paper next to his pillow. The paper said, "It is 5:00 a.m. Wake up."

# 770

One day, while out at recess, two boys noticed that a van began rolling down the parking lot with no one in the driver's seat. They quickly ran to the vehicle, jumped in, and put on the emergency brake. Seconds later, the door opened and there was the principal, his face red with anger. "What's going on?" he asked.

"We stopped this van from rolling away," said one of the boys.

The principal, huffing and sweaty, said, "I know. It stalled, and I was pushing it."

# 771

A flight attendant was on the red-eye to Miami when a water leak developed in the galley, which eventually soaked the carpet throughout the cabin of the aircraft.

A very tired passenger who had become aware of the dampness asked the attendant, "Has it been raining?"

Keeping a straight face, the attendant replied, "Yes, but we put the top up."

With a sigh of relief, the passenger drifted off to sleep.

# 772

A newly hired flight attendant was preparing for his first flight. He was a bit nervous, dropping trays and spilling drinks on passengers.

"Calm down," said his coworker. "You're acting as if you've never flown before."

"Oh, I've *flown* many times," he said. "But just before takeoff, I looked all around the plane. After that, I had a terrible panic attack."

"Why? It's just another aircraft."

"But I realized every part was supplied by the lowest bidder."

## 773

One day a father was driving with his five-year-old daughter, when he honked his car horn by mistake.

"I did that by accident," he said.

"I know that, Daddy," she replied.

"How did you know that?"

"Because you didn't holler at the other driver after you honked it."

## 774

The flight attendant was pointing out to the passengers that their seats could be removed and used as a flotation device. One man, flying for the first time, commented, "I'd prefer to be sitting on a parachute."

## 775

"What papers do I need for my trip to England?" a college student asked the travel agent.

"A passport and a visa," was the reply.

"I already have the passport, but. . .do you think they'd accept MasterCard?"

# 776

A man riding a bike and carrying two sacks on his shoulders was stopped by a guard while crossing the border.

"What do you have in those bags?" asked the guard.

"Sand," the cyclist replied.

"You'll need to open them so I can take a look inside."

The guard emptied the bags and found out they did indeed contain nothing but sand. The man put his bags back on his shoulders and continued across the border.

This happened a couple of times each week for a month. Sometime later, that same guard ran into the cyclist in the city.

"Hey, where have you been?" the guard asked. "You sure had me wondering. I know you were smuggling something across the border. If you tell me what it was, I won't prosecute you. What was it?"

The man smiled and said, "Bicycles!"

# 777

A passenger train slowly crept along. Finally it creaked to a halt. A passenger saw the conductor outside and called to him, "What's going on?"

"There's a cow on the tracks!" answered the conductor.

Fifteen minutes later, the train once again began creeping down the tracks. Within a few minutes, however, it stopped again.

The woman saw the conductor outside the window again. She leaned out the window and yelled, "What happened? Did we catch up with the cow?"

# Joke Books from Barbour Publishing

*Noah's Favorite Animal Jokes*
JENNIFER HAHN
Categorized by animal—this book is packed with hilarious, crazy, and/or corny stories, riddles, and one-liners appropriate for anyone. 240 pages
1-58660-995-5

*The Teacher, Teacher Joke Book*
JENNIFER HAHN
With hundreds of jokes from elementary, junior high, high school, college—even Sunday school—this collection is sure to bring back memories and make you laugh. 240 pages
1-59310-138-4

*The World's Greatest Collection of Church Jokes*
PAUL M. MILLER
This hilarious collection contains scores of funnies involving pastors, deacons, Sunday school teachers, pew sitters, and kids—all of them clean, funny, and good-natured. 256 pages
1-59310-018-3